The Bodybuilding Bible for Men

The ultimate guidebook to building men's muscles in a short time. A book that explains effective training exercises and proper bodybuilding nutrients plan for males

Henrik Mulford

Table of Contents

Table of Contents

Introduction

Chapter 1: The Perfect Diet for Bodybuilders

   What is Bulking?

   What is Cutting?
      The Right Amount of Calories during The Bulking Phase
      The Right Amount of Calories during the Cutting Phase

   Macronutrient Ratio

   What you Should Eat, What you Should Avoid

   Foods you should Cut-down

   Foods you should Avoid Just before Training

   Can Bodybuilders Take Supplements?

   Factors to Consider When Bodybuilding

   10 Best Foods for Muscle Growth

   Chapter 1 Summary

Chapter 2: Setting Goals and Achieving Them

   Long-term Goals vs Short-term Goals

   How Do You Measure Your Progress?

   7 Practical Steps You Can Take To Reach Your Goals

How to Stop Yourself from Skipping Training Sessions

The Benefits of Training in Groups

Disadvantages of Training in Groups

Bodybuilding Budget
The Building Blocks Food
The Supplements
Gym, Workout Gear, and Equipment Costs

Chapter 2 Summary

Chapter 3: How to Build Muscle Mass Effectively

8 Ways to Effectively Build Mass

Do I Need a Private Trainer To Build My Muscles?
Questions You Need To Ask Yourself Before You Hire a Private Trainer

Best Weight Training Programs
The 5X5 Program
German Volume Training
The FST-7 Training Program
Upper/Lower Split Training

Chapter 3 Summary

Chapter 4: How to Use the Gym, Fitness & Other Exercise Tools at Home

Pros of Training at Home

Cons of Training at Home

Equipment You Will Need To Train At Home

How to Use Adjustable Dumbbells
What You Will Need

Adjustable Dumbbells Vs Fixed Dumbbells
- Pros of Using Adjustable Dumbbells
- Cons of Using Adjustable Dumbbells
- Pros of Using Fixed Dumbbells
- Cons of Using Fixed Dumbbells

How to Use a Bench with Incline Adjustments
- How to Do the Incline Bench Press-Form and Technique
- Incline Bench Press-Muscles Worked
- Benefits of the Incline Bench Press
- Who Should Do the Inclined Bench Press?
- Inclined Bench Press Sets, Reps, and Weight Recommendations
- Inclined Bench Press Variations

How to Use a Chin-up Bar
- Benefits
- Step-by-step Instructions
- Common Mistakes
- Modifications and Variations
- Extra Challenge?
- Safety and Precautions

How to Use a Squat Rack
- Full Body Squat Rack Workout
- Exercise You Can Do With a Squat Rack

How Often Should I Increase Weights on Squats

What Determines How Often We Can Train (When Bodybuilding)

What Determines Training Frequency?
- MPS Rate
- Muscle Damage

Food For Thought

Chapter 4 Summary

Chapter 5: Proven Models That Successful Bodybuilders Use

Pro Bodybuilder Physique
Training Program Weeks 1-6
Training Program Weeks 7-12
Diet Strategy Weeks 1-12

How Do Pro Bodybuilders Track Their Progress
Maximizing Your Training
Tracking Your Progress: Measuring Body Composition
Quick Recap: Ways to Measure Body Composition Progress

The Taylor Lautner Workout: Build Muscle Fast
The Lautner's Formula for a 6-pack

Mike Tyson's Diet and Nutrition

Anthony Joshua's Diet Plan

Top 10 Bodybuilding Supplements That Work
How to Avoid Supplement Overdose and Misleading Bodybuilding Mistakes
A word of Caution When Using Supplements
5 Natural Supplements You Need for Real Muscle Gains
How to Build Muscle without Supplements

Chapter 5 Summary

Chapter 6: Bodybuilding Myths

Myths about Building Arms

Myths about Weight Loss

Chapter 6 Summary

Chapter 7: How to Boost Hormones

8 Testosterone-Boosting Foods
More Food for Thought

Growth Hormone Deficiency
What Causes Growth Hormone Deficiency
Symptoms of Growth Hormone Deficiency
How is Growth Hormone Deficiency Diagnosed?
How is Growth Hormone Deficiency Treated?

How to Stimulate Hormones for Bodybuilding
- Key Hormones in Bodybuilding
- How to Enhance Hormones Naturally
- Foods that Lower Testosterone Levels
- The Bottom Line

Chapter 7 Summary

Chapter 8: How to Dress to Match Your New Body

Suit Buying Tips for Muscular Men

Jeans Buying Tips for Men with Muscular Thighs
- The Problem
- Getting the Right Fit for Jeans
- Best Jeans for Muscular Legs
- Food for Thought

T-shirts for Bodybuilders

Chapter 8 Summary

Conclusion

Introduction

In today's world, more and more men are taking up the hobby of bodybuilding. Could it be for health or competitive reasons, could it be to impress that hot chick in your neighborhood, or do you just want to look fabulous when you dress to an event?

Whatever your reasons are, it's a step in the right direction!

Looking good as they say, is good business. The better your body is shaped, the better you will feel about yourself, and the more confident you will be.

We understand this, and that's the reason we have put this guide together, specially for you. It will give you very informative body-building tips, both in the region of physical work-outs, and proper dieting.

Chapter 1: The Perfect Diet for Bodybuilders

The first step to looking and feeling good is eating right. If you plan to build-up your body the right way, then you have to eat right too!

So, what should bodybuilders eat, and in what quantities?

For those who don't know, bodybuilding training and dieting are split into two parts. These are:

- The bulking phase
- The cutting phase

What is Bulking?

Bulking is the first phase of bodybuilding. Here, the bodybuilder aims to build up muscles, and he does this by going on certain diets and engaging in specific muscle-building exercises.

The bulking phase could take years to complete. Within this period, the bodybuilder eats foods that are high in calories and protein, and they also engage in very intense work-outs.

What is Cutting?

The second phase of bodybuilding is called cutting. This phase is when the bodybuilder tries to lose as much fat as possible while maintaining the muscles that have been built-up over time.

During this stage, the bodybuilder's diet has to change, and the work-out routines have to be adjusted.

The amount of calories consumed in the cutting phase is significantly less than the amount consumed in the bulking phase.

It takes about 15 to 20 weeks for the cutting phase to be completed, provided the bodybuilder follows the outline diligently.

The Right Amount of Calories during The Bulking Phase

As I mentioned earlier, you will need to eat foods that are high in calories during the bulking phase, but what amount exactly do you need?

Individuals are of different sizes, so it's tough to put a finger on a specific number. However, you can weigh yourself 2 to 3 times weekly to be sure of what you weigh.

If your weight remains the same after several checks, it means the number of calories you are consuming is at maintenance level.

Remember, the purpose of bulking is to build muscles, not to lose or maintain it.

Therefore, I advise (as many other experts would), that you increase your calorie intake by 15%. This means if at maintenance level, you consume 4,000 calories daily, then you should up it by 15%, which will amount to 4,600 calories per day.

How are you going to measure your calories? You may ask. Well, there are several calorie-tracking apps you could use to be certain of the number of calories you consume.

The Right Amount of Calories during the Cutting Phase

The cutting phase is where you're trying to burn all the unwanted fat while retaining the muscles you developed during the bulking phase.

What this means is a reduction in the number of calories being consumed. The same amount of 15% is appropriate.

So, if your maintenance level of calories consumed is 4,000 per day, a 15% reduction would amount to 3,400 calories per day.

As your body-weight changes, during both the bulking phase and cutting phase, you will need to make monthly adjustments to your calorie intake.

As you gain weight during the bulking phase, you should increase your calorie intake by 0.5 to 1% every month. Also, as you lose weight during the cutting phase, you should reduce your calorie intake by 0.5 to 1% every month.

This will ensure you don't lose or gain too much weight in either of these phases.

Macronutrient Ratio

Now that you've determined the number of calories you will need during your quest for a great body, it's time to figure out the macronutrient ratio you will need.

The term "macronutrient ratio" sounds more complicated than it actually is. It simply means the ration between protein, carbohydrates, and fat consumption.

Your macronutrient ratio, unlike your calorie intake during the bulking and cutting stages, does not change. It remains constant all-through your bodybuilding process.

In carbohydrates and protein, you can find 4 calories per gram. As for fats, you can find 9 calories per gram.

Below is the recommended macronutrient ratio:

- 35% of your calories (from protein)
- 55% of your calories (from carbohydrates)
- 15% of your calories (from fats)

Keep in mind that the above percentages are just estimates, so you can consume amounts around the above figures.

What you Should Eat, What you Should Avoid

So, I think it's time we get into the specifics. Being an aspiring bodybuilder, or a bodybuilder in the making, what foods, in particular, should you eat, and what foods should you shun?

Keep in mind that consuming the wrong foods, or the right foods in the wrong amounts will lead you to poor results.

Here's what you need to eat.

Try some meat and fish: A combination of meat and fish will do you some good in your bodybuilding ambitions.

The kinds of meat ideal for you include steak, salmon, chicken breast, cods, and pork

Dairy is always an option: What would a bodybuilder's diet be without some cheese, low-fat milk, and yogurt? I recommend!

Grains are good too: You could have some rice, cereal, oatmeal, and bread.

Let's not forget the fruits: Fruits are one of the most important parts of a bodybuilder's diet. They are natural detoxifiers, and they are really refreshing.

You can try some oranges, apples, watermelons, bananas, and pears.

They will do you so much good!

Also try starchy vegetables: These are good too. You can try some great peas, beans, potatoes, corn, and green lima.

Throw in some seeds and nuts: Almonds, walnuts, sunflower seeds, and flax seeds.

Beans and legumes: Kidney beans, black beans, pinto beans, chickpeas, and lentils.

Foods you should Cut-down

As there are foods that can help you build up your muscles in a healthy manner, there are also foods that can limit muscle growth.

We will be looking at these foods below.

Alcoholic beverages: Alcohol, if consumed excessively, can limit muscle growth. Too much alcohol can also slow the process by which you lose fat.

It's a terrible idea to drink heavily while in your bodybuilding stages.

Foods with added sugars: Such foods include cake, candy, sweets, sweetened drinks, sodas, and sports drinks. These foods may be high in calories, but they are seriously lacking in nutrients.

Deep-fried foods: These include French fries, deep-fried chicken, fried fish, and cheese curds.

These types of foods are dangerous when consumed excessively. They do not only promote inflammation, but they can also lead to heart disease.

Keep in mind that there are certain foods you need to avoid eating before starting your day's training. Such foods can upset your stomach and leave you with a horrible workout experience.

Foods you should Avoid Just before Training

Below is a list of foods you should avoid before you start your training.

High-fat foods: These include fatty creams, fatty meats, and buttery food.

These are terrible foods to consume just before you hit the gym. Generally, excess consumption of fatty foods has several cardiovascular disadvantages.

High-fiber foods: Try as much as you can to avoid cruciferous vegetables before going to the gym.

Cruciferous vegetables include broccoli and cauliflower. Also, avoid eating beans.

Carbonated beverages: You would be doing yourself a huge favor by dodging carbonated drinks as you hit the gym.

Carbonated drinks carry a lot of gas, which will keep you uncomfortable throughout your training session.

Can Bodybuilders Take Supplements?

Sure, bodybuilders have been taking supplements for decades. Some of them are effective, while others are nothing but a waste of time.

Recommended supplements for bodybuilders include the following:

Whey Protein: If you're in need of a protein-boost, and you don't think the proteins in your regular diet are enough, then you can consume Whey protein powder.

It can add the extra protein you need.

Creatine: Creatine can give you a super energy boost. If you're game for an extra set with your training buddies, then this might be good for you.

I recommend Creatine monohydrate, as it has proven to be very effective.

Caffeine: This is another great workout supplement. It helps you eliminate fatigue and it charges you to put in more work.

You can find caffeine in some supplements, but most commonly in coffee.

If you are in your cutting phase (the phase where you're trying to lose fat), then it would be a good idea to take multi-vitamins and mineral supplements, since you're already cutting down your calorie intake.

Factors to Consider When Bodybuilding

Many bodybuilding experts and professionals call it a "religion", some call it a "culture", you know why? Because it is something that is to be done every day, which automatically makes it a way of life.

As we know with all daily habits, we will be shaped, both mentally and physically by what we practice every day.

That being said, bodybuilding also has a way of shaping not just our bodies, but our minds and lives as well.

Below, I'd like to point out some factors you need to take into consideration before you start bodybuilding.

Keep reading!

1. Low Levels Of Body Fat Can Affect Your Sleep And Mood

Research has shown that low levels of body fat can affect the way a person sleeps, and their mood in general.

Others have shown that bodybuilders who are in preparation for competitions can cut down their body fat to as low as 10% to 15%.

Such levels are dangerously low, as it can lead to sleepless nights, awful mood-swings, and can affect your relationship with those close to you.

Another danger that comes with a lack of sleep is the weakening of the immune system. This would over-time, leave one susceptible to chronic illnesses.

I know you'd like to look great, but you don't have to burn out all the fat from your body to do so. Fat still has an important role to play in the human body, so let's keep a substantial amount in reserve ok?

2. Risk Of Using Anabolic Steroids

There are a lot of muscle-building supplements being advertised by bodybuilders who use performance-enhancing drugs. Such drugs include anabolic steroids.

Those who are new to the world of bodybuilding could be easily misled by these adverts, thinking it's the supplements that are responsible for the model's shape, unaware that anabolic steroids are responsible.

The newbies who watch these adverts would be prompted to buy the supplements but would be very disappointed when they don't achieve the same results as those they see on the adverts.

This could lead them into the temptation of trying out steroids too. Unfortunately, this is a temptation many bodybuilders have fallen for.

At this point of temptation, many new bodybuilders forget that they can achieve the desired physique by natural means.

The use (or abuse) of steroids always backfires in the long run, being that it is very unhealthy and it carries several side-effects along with it.

These dangerous side effects include:

- Loss of fertility (inability to make babies)
- Increase in risk of mental disorders
- Increase in risk of heart disease

Are these risks worth it? The obvious answer is no. Anabolic steroids cause more harm than good.

Before I forget, I have to mention that owning anabolic steroids without prescription is illegal in America. You see, it really isn't worth it.

There is no physique you want for your body that you cannot achieve on your own, naturally.

Don't be lazy, let's go for it!

10 Best Foods for Muscle Growth

What's bodybuilding without the addition of muscles, and how can you effectively add muscles without eating muscle-building foods?

Keep reading, as I will be taking you through 10 of the best foods for muscle growth.

Stay with me!

1. Quinoa

This is a grain that can be found mainly in the South American regions. It is very rich and protein and it is ideal for men who don't fancy eating meat.

Another health benefit of quinoa is that it contains all 9 essential amino acids. It is also high in fiber and extremely easy to digest.

According to the ancient Inca tribe of South America, the Quinoa is popularly called the "Mother of all grains".

2. Almonds

It would interest you to know that 1/4 cup of almonds contains as much as 8 grams of muscle-growing proteins. If you think about how the "almighty" egg contains only about 6 grams of protein, then I think you would want to give the almond a lot more respect, as a protein-rich muscle-builder.

Besides being rich in protein, almonds are also rich in monounsaturated fats and magnesium.

3. Cottage Cheese

If you are a bodybuilder and you do not include cottage cheese in your diet, then you are missing out on one of the greatest natural muscle-builders in the world!

Amazingly, 1/2 a cup of low-fat cottage cheese is loaded with up to 14 grams of protein in less than 80 calories, and let than 2 grams of fat.

They are healthy, they help build muscles fast, and they are rich in protein. Need I say more?

4. Oysters

20 grams of protein and less than 5 grams of fat is what 100 grams of cooked Pacific oysters would offer you.

Oh, they also contain more zinc than any other food known to man. Remember, zinc is an essential mineral for protein synthesis.

That being said, there is no surprise that oysters are very popular among bodybuilders around the world.

5. Milk

This also is a popular source of pure, natural protein.

One of the biggest advantages of milk is that it is an animal food, so it contains all the essential amino acids you would need for muscle growth. It is low in fat too!

Remember **Whey Protein**? I mentioned it earlier in this book, well it mixes very well with milk. Think of all the low-fat, protein goodness you'll be getting from such a beverage!

It's a bodybuilder's dream combination!

6. Lean Ground Beef

Yes, I know, there is a "red meat stigma" when it comes to beef, but they aren't all that bad. Lean ground beef is an excellent source of protein, which helps build your muscles.

In just 100 grams of lean ground beef, you can find protein in excess of 27 grams.

As packed as it is with protein, it is equally packed with fat and calories, and that is the only downside for me.

100 grams of lean ground beef contains 11 grams of fat and a whopping 200 calories.

That aside, it also contains high volumes of much-needed vitamin B12, Iron, and Zinc. All three of these are essential to muscle growth, and this is why lean ground beef remains a top choice food for those who want to build their muscles!

7. Soy

When it comes to plant sources of protein, there aren't too many that can top soy!

Besides protein, soy is packed with other healthy vitamins and minerals that the human body needs to grow.

A cooked cup of this protein-rich food can give you up to 20 grams of muscle-building amino acids.

It remains a popular choice among weightlifters, fitness instructors, and bodybuilders.

8. Eggs

What would this list be if eggs were not on it? It doesn't get more popular than this!

A regular-sized egg comes with about 6 grams of protein, and a very low amount of calories (60 calories).

The thing that makes egg-protein so special isn't just the amount of protein found in it, it's also the type of protein in has.

According to research, egg protein is the most readily-utilizable protein you can find in any food.

This makes it one of the best foods you can consume for the sake of building those muscles of yours!

9. Chicken

Check this out, 100 grams of chicken will give you about 31 grams of protein, and only 4 grams of fat.

This makes chicken one of the best foods as far as food/protein/fat ratio is concerned.

When you think of how delicious chicken is, along with its versatility in meals, and its muscle-building capabilities, one could argue that chicken is the greatest protein-giving food of them all.

10. Fish

The only protein giving animal that can give chicken a run for its money is fish!

Fish isn't just rich in protein, it also contains healthy fats and oils. They taste great too!

Salmon and Tuna fish rank among the healthiest fish one can consume.

A 100 gram serving of Salmon will give you 25 grams of protein, but that's not where it stops! Salmon also contains Vitamin D, Omega-3 fatty acids, and monounsrated fats.

As far as building muscles is concerned, there aren't too many foods out there that can topple fish.

Just like chicken, fish is also delicious and can be served with a variety of dishes. They can also be found everywhere around the globe. I really can't think of a country that doesn't have fish!

Chapter 1 Summary

As we discussed at the beginning of this chapter, eating the right foods in the right amounts will help your body look and feel better.

Remember, there are stages to bodybuilding, the bulking stage, and the cutting stage. You have to patiently pass through these stages by sticking to the right diets. There are no "instant" results in bodybuilding.

There are also special foods you need to add to your diet that will help you build your muscles in a natural, healthy way.

That being said, and hopefully understood, I'd like us to proceed to the next chapter.

Here we will discuss the importance of knowing and understanding your body, and how to set realistic targets for yourself.

Keep reading!

Chapter 2: Setting Goals and Achieving Them

Many newcomers into the world of bodybuilding make the mistake of not setting realistic goals and working towards them.

It is common to hear them say things like *"I want to look like XXX in the next two weeks"*, and they end up getting disappointed after the two-week period when they look in the mirror and don't see any changes.

This is where setting realistic personal goals come in. Truthfully, you can't start bodybuilding today and expect to look like a world-class athlete in 2 weeks. Impossible!

The unnecessary rush to be buff has led many towards the direction of steroids, which of course cause more harm than good.

So, how do you set realistic goals for yourself, and how do you stick to them?

Keep reading, as I will give you simple tips on how you can set these goals, and achieve them.

Long-term Goals vs Short-term Goals

For a bodybuilder, setting goals is everything, both short-term and long-term.

It is the long-term goals that influence the short-term training efforts, and it is the short-term training that leads to achieving the long-term goals.

For a bodybuilder, his long-term goals may be to look better for the next competition, 1 or 2 years away. Progress or a change in his looks over-time may not seem obvious, being that he is already a trained bodybuilder, but his short-term improvements can show how well he has done.

These short-term improvements may be an increase in the amount of weight he carries or an improved resistance level during training.

Such short-term improvements (which can be measured), is what will keep you on-track in the quest to achieving your long-term goals.

No matter how motivated or disciplined a bodybuilder is, he may lose focus on his long-term goals. This is why setting short-term goals in-between is very important.

The bottom line is, it would be very difficult to achieve long-term goals without setting short-term goals along the line.

We all need reassurance along the line, just to remain motivated to continue, and being able to carry an extra 10kg after every month of training can be pretty reassuring.

How Do You Measure Your Progress?

A lot of professional bodybuilders measure their progress by how well they rank in the next competition. This isn't bad, but if we're being realistic, there are other factors that will determine your placing at the contest.

These factors include:

- How good you look
- The judges' opinions
- How good the other contestants look

Out of these 3 factors, how many do you have control over? My answer is as good as yours, just one!

How you look is the only factor you have control over in a contest, there's really nothing you can do to control the other factors. This is why for a pro bodybuilder, using ranking in a competition to measure progress is a bad idea.

There are better ways to measure your progress.

These include:

1. Improved Weightlifting Ability

Set a target of how much extra weight you would like to be able to lift in the coming months. Track how much extra weight you are strong enough to lift every month, and if you see you've gone from lifting 50kg to 52kg for example, then that's a big improvement.

2. Fat Reduction

Another way to track your progress is by taking records of your fat levels.

So how do you know that you're burning fat? There are a few simple ways to measure this.

- Increased physical energy
- Clothes fit more loosely
- Reduced cravings for candy and other sweets

3. Increase In Training Time

This is another way by which you can determine if you are making progress or not.

When you notice you are putting in extra minutes, or even an hour into training, it means you are making some really good progress.

Don't forget to be realistic about this. If you're a beginner, you can't expect to go from training for 1 hour every 3 days, to training for 3 hours every 5 days within one month.

All levels of progress are welcome. Remember, slow progress is better than no progress.

That being said, I'd like to list out 7 practical steps you can take to reach your goals.

7 Practical Steps You Can Take To Reach Your Goals

For every dream to turn to reality, there are steps that must be followed. Nothing worth achieving happens by mistake.

It will take a clear line of action to do so. The actions must also be realistic!

What are these practical steps that will take you to the "promised land" of physical awesomeness?

Keep reading!

1. Set Long-term Goals

Knowing exactly what you want to achieve over the next 12 months will help you plan the right steps to helping you achieve it.

Maybe you want to gain or lose an extra 40 pounds by this time next year. Write it down and start working towards it.

Place that piece of paper on your wall, fridge door, or anywhere else you are sure you look at every day. This will on a daily basis, remind you of your commitment to improving your physical looks.

By determining your long-term goals, you will know exactly where you're going (training-wise), it also means you can figure out the right path to follow to achieving these goals.

2. Set Short-term Goals

So, you've set a long-term target of losing (or gaining) 40 pounds over 12 months. Guess what? You won't lose or gain that weight just because you wrote it down on a piece of paper and placed it on your wall.

This is where your short-term goals come in. These are the achievable steps you can take on a day-to-day basis that will help you meet your long-term target.

For instance, you can decide to lose (or gain) one pound per week. Yes, it could be more, but I'd like us to speak realistically.

Setting realistic short-term targets and sticking to the plan is the only way you can achieve your long-term goals.

As I said before, slow progress is better than no progress!

3. Make Your Goals Measurable

The only realistic way you can tell if you're making progress is when you can measure your efforts.

You can jump on a scale at the end of every week to see your results. If you've not lost or added the desired weight, then you can make some adjustments to your daily diet.

You can speak to your personal trainer or dietician to help you determine what foods you need to start or stop eating, and by what quantities.

Being able to measure your progress will allow you hold yourself accountable, hence, set you on a path to achieving both short and long-term goals.

4. Don't Be Too Hard On Yourself

A lot of people tend to want that perfect body right now, however, a well-carved physique doesn't manifest at the push of a button!

Getting that ultimate body takes time, and you must give yourself enough time to achieve your dream.

Don't over-work yourself during training in a bid to get there quickly, because you won't.

Your body needs time to respond to training and diet. Doing a "million" bench-presses in a day doesn't mean you'll wake up the next morning looking like Christiano Ronaldo.

The danger of setting unrealistic targets is that it can lead to frustration when the desired results are not achieved. We all know what frustration can do, it could actually can you to give up on your dreams all-together!

5. Follow the Plan

When you come up with a plan that works for you, I advise you stick to it.

If your aim is to lose or gain one pound per week, and your workout plan is getting the job done, then continue with it.

As the months go by, you would have improved greatly, and at that point, you can make a minor adjustment to your workout plans.

For instance, at the beginning stages, you could be training 2 hours a day, 3 days a week. In the fourth or fifth month, you can up your training-time by 30 minutes. This would mean training for 2hrs 30mins a day, 3 days a week.

6. Be Your Own Motivation

If you're going into bodybuilding for the sake of impressing others, then you will likely fail, or give up when the people you are trying to impress are gone.

For this reason, you need to be your own motivation. The best way to succeed at anything in life (not just bodybuilding), is to do it for yourself.

If bodybuilding doesn't make you happy or is something you don't really want to do for your own sake, then I suggest you call it quits.

This is not to say you should walk the road alone, of course not! Actually, it would be a great idea if you train with people who are equally motivated to do it for themselves. Watching others work hard for themselves will encourage you to do the same.

7. Reward Yourself

There's nothing that would encourage a person to keep up the good work more than a reward. In this case, it's up to you to reward yourself.

You know how it is when you receive a bonus at work for a well-executed project, or how the doctor gives a child candy for being well-behaved during check-ups? That's exactly how it should be when you reach certain milestones in your training.

Let's say you really don't like broccoli, but you have to include it in your diet for fitness-sake, you can substitute it for something you enjoy eating, but equally healthy (maybe in a meal or two). Green beans for instance.

You could also take yourself out to see a movie, or engage in any other activity you enjoy when you hit certain milestones in your training.

Remember not to indulge in destructive habits and use that as an excuse for a reward. Going all-out on a large steak isn't the kind of reward I am talking about, neither is drinking excessively nor smoking!

How to Stop Yourself from Skipping Training Sessions

We are all human, and having shortcomings here and there is expected every now and then.

This can also be the case with a person in training.

You may skip one or two training sessions this week, and maybe one session the next week. Maybe yesterday, you trained for only 45 minutes instead of 2 hours.

This happens to a lot of people, so don't be surprised if it happens to you.

However, you will not achieve your short or long-term goals if you keep skipping training.

So, what do you do when you find yourself slacking?

The tips I will give you below will help you stay on track!

1. Remind yourself why you're Doing This In The First Place

Constantly reminding yourself why you got into bodybuilding in the first place is a great way to keep you on track with your training sessions, and even your diet.

The "reason" will likely encourage the "action".

When you're reminded why you need to hit the gym, and the benefits it will bring, you will be motivated to get out of bed and go for the dumbbells!

Here's an extra tip: You can write out all the good reasons you have to work out on a piece of paper, or set reminders on your smartphone.

Having these constant reminders will prick your conscience anytime you feel lazy about working out.

2. Buy Pricey Workout Gear

This may seem a bit too extravagant, but I guess you'll feel terrible when you see all your expensive workout gear lying around when you're supposed to be putting them to good use.

For those who don't have a budget for expensive gear, you can buy the fairly-priced ones that you like.

Buy your favorite brand of training shoes, make sure the ones you buy come in your favorite color too. The fact that you enjoy wearing them will help you stay committed to training. Where else would you wear them to if not the gym, a wedding?

This psychological tactic has proven to be very effective. It's like when you buy a new jacket, or a brand new pair of Jordan sneakers, you'd just want to put them on and go somewhere befitting.

That's exactly the same effect you'd get when you buy expensive workout gear or workout gear that you love!

3. Become Friends with Those Who Are Regular In Training Sessions

I'm sure there will be more than enough nice folks at the gym where you train. I suggest you make friends with them, as they could be vital to helping you keep up with training.

Exchange phone numbers with them, follow each other on Instagram, be friends on Facebook, set up WhatsApp groups etc. Once in a while, you guys can all go out to see a game, or attend any other healthy social activity.

If for any reason you miss a training session, guess who's going to call you? Your training buddies!

That's how simple this trick is!

As I mentioned earlier, you may skip one or two sessions out of laziness, but when your gym pals start checking up on you, then you will be more motivated to get up and go.

Knowing that you're slacking at home, and they are out there chasing their bodybuilding goals will make you feel like a loser. That feeling hurts!

4. Set up A Challenge among Yourselves

Another way to stay consistent with training is to set up challenges among yourselves.

It could be a one-month consistency challenge, where the most diligent member for a whole month gets rewarded by other members of the class. In the same vein, the most inconsistent member could face a light punishment (maybe he would have to buy lunch for everyone).

Of course, this would be based on friendly agreements between you and your gym members. However, nobody wants to lose at a game, so this can help you stay consistent with training.

5. Make Workout Sessions a Fun Experience

My last tip for you regarding workout consistency is to make each workout session as fun as possible.

When you have fun doing something, you will always want to repeat the process. If you do not enjoy your training sessions, you will be discouraged from attending further trainings.

On the other hand, if your training sessions are fun, you wouldn't want to miss the next one.

Yeah I know, bodybuilding is serious business, but what's a physical workout session without some good music and some laughs?

Have your favorite songs arranged in a playlist, and dedicate it to your workout sessions. You and your workout buddies could vote on which playlist will be used during the next session, and so on.

After your workouts, you guys can also take some pictures and upload them to your social media pages and your WhatsApp groups.

Scrolling through your feed and seeing all the pictures you guys took from the last session would spur you to be a part of the next session. Something else that would encourage you is the likes and comments from your social media followers and friends.

The Benefits of Training in Groups

I mentioned earlier how having workout pals can help you stay consistent with attending training sessions, but that's not the only advantage to it.

Training in groups has many other advantages, and I will look at them one by one.

Before I do, I'd like to give you some statistical facts about training in groups.

Several studies have revealed that about 95% of people who start weight-loss programs with their friends end up finishing the program. Research has also shown that only 25% of people who embark on weight-loss programs alone actually finish it.

Other studies have revealed that training with a more capable partner can increase your efficiency by 24%. Lastly, a study on obese individuals showed that overweight people who spend a lot of time with their fit friends end up losing weight.

This is the power of training in groups!

That being said, I'd like us to go deeper into the major advantages of training with a group.

1. You Will Be Motivated To Do Better

Imagine if you could do 20 push-ups per rep, but every other member of your group can do 30 to 35 push-ups per rep. How would that make you feel, knowing you all started bodybuilding the same time?

The feeling of being last is not nice, as you can imagine. For this reason, you will be motivated to do more and keep up with your mates.

This is not to say you should over-work yourself, being that you guys may not even be of the same body-size or strength, but the motivation it brings is one that will be beneficial to your long and short-term bodybuilding goals.

2. Group Members Can Help You Train Better

Have you ever been in the middle of your push-ups, and your training buddy stops you and says, *"Hey, you're doing it wrong"*?

This is a very common occurrence with people who train in groups. They help each other out by pointing out each other's mistakes during training.

It could be your squats, bench press, push-ups, weightlifting, etc.

Whatever it is, members of your group can act as your extra eyes, and help you spot and correct your mistakes.

3. Group Training Is More Fun

They say two's a company and three is a crowd, but what about four or five? I guess that's a party!

When you train in groups, you have more people to share fun moments with, which I would not have been possible if you trained alone.

Remember, the more fun you have with your training, the better you will feel, and the more you would want to attend subsequent sessions.

4. Group Training Helps You Stay Consistent

Training with groups will keep you motivated to attend sessions regularly. If your gym buddies attend training classes consistently, you wouldn't want to disappoint them by not showing up.

Disadvantages of Training in Groups

As beneficial as group training can be, it also comes with its fair share of downsides.

Bodybuilding is a personal thing, meaning it should be all about you (as selfish as that may sound).

I'd like to list out the major disadvantages of training in a group.

1. You Cannot Have Your Trainer's Full Attention

This is the first problem with group-training. When your trainer is monitoring several individuals at the same time, he wouldn't be able to focus on you alone.

When you do a routine the wrong way, your trainer might miss it, and won't be able to correct you. It's true that one of your group members can correct you, but he is not the trainer, and his correction may not be as effective as that of the main trainer who is qualified for the job.

2. The Individual's Needs Are Not Customized

You may weigh 300 pounds when you start your training, and another member of your group could weigh 250 pounds at the start. Your weight isn't the problem here, it's how your trainer would meet your unique needs that would be challenging.

Being that each member of the group differs in weight, having a general routine may not be the most effective.

The diet adjustments of a 300-pound man should differ from a man who weighs 200 pounds. The exercise routines should be different too.

Not being able to customize your training routine to your body's specific needs is one of the biggest disadvantages of group-training.

3. You May Want To Be Shaped Like One Of Your Group Members

It's easy for people to be influenced by what they constantly see. A member of your group may be shaped a certain way, and you may be influenced to take-on workout routines that you believe will make you look the same way.

This is a bad idea because it means you will stop your already-existing routine and diet which has been working for you over the past week or months.

If you do this, you will not achieve your short-term and long-term goals. On the contrary, you will end up with less-than-satisfactory results.

Bodybuilding Budget

So far, we have spoken about the best muscle-building foods, as well as how to stay motivated and committed to hitting the gym regularly.

The thing is, both food and gym membership isn't free!

These will cost you a decent sum of money (nobody said bodybuilding was cheap).

As you embark on your bodybuilding journey, you need to draw up a budget to cater for the expenses that will come along the way.

You will need money for the special diets, the supplements, gym registration & membership, and of course, work out gear.

You may wonder how much you need to set aside for this on a weekly, monthly, or annual basis. Well, I will give you a breakdown of what you will need to spend money on, and how much it might cost you.

Keep reading, as the information I am about to provide is very essential to achieving your bodybuilding goals.

The Building Blocks Food

A reasonable amount of money to spend on food per week falls within the $100 range.

You could spend less, maybe around $80, but a $100 budget will do just fine.

Keep in mind that besides the regular diet, you may come across some healthy, protein-filled, mouth-watering fish that you just can't say no to.

Here's how the $100 budget could be spent.

- 5lbs chicken breast - $20.00
- 10 cans tuna - $10.00
- 2-3 gallons milk - $8.00
- 1 pound cold cuts - $8.00
- 2 dozen eggs - $5.00
- A loaf of wheat bread - $2.50
- A pound of almonds - $6.00
- A box of brown rice - $4.00
- 20 servings of oats - $4.00
- Vegetables - $10.00
- Fruits - $15.00

The above listed totals about $90, you'll still have an extra $10 left from your $100 budget.

Between the meat and eggs, you will have over 1,000 grams of protein per week.

So, on a $100 budget, you can have delicious, healthy, protein-rich, organic food every week.

The Supplements

Most bodybuilders would tell you that the budget for supplements can be as low as zero, or as high as $1,000.

There are so many supplements out there and you may be tempted to try out more than necessary.

Here's a general breakdown of how much you can expect to spend if you decide to take supplements.

- 5lbs of whey protein - $40.00
- 90 ZMA capsules - $10.00
- 200g Creatine - $10.00 (you can buy this in bulk easily!)
- 100g fish oil - $15.00
- Multivitamin - $8.00

Your reasons for bodybuilding can also determine the number of supplements you need, and how much you would be spending on them.

For instance, a person who is bodybuilding for sport would want to spend more on supplements than a person who is bodybuilding for the sake of looking fit.

Generally speaking, on behalf of the average bodybuilder, spending $200 a month seems about right.

Gym, Workout Gear, and Equipment Costs

If you plan on training at home, then you would need to invest in some training equipment. These would include the bench, weights, dumbbells etc.

The good thing about this is that you only need to buy the equipment once, and you'll use it for as long as it can serve (which is usually a pretty long time).

However, if you plan to register at a gym, then you wouldn't need to buy any equipment for your home. Nonetheless, gym today membership isn't free, so you'll also have to part with some money.

The thing about gym membership is that it expires, which means you have to renew it. It could be on a monthly or yearly basis.

The cost of gym membership depends on the area where the gym is located, and the status they have attained in the bodybuilding & fitness industry.

Gyms in rural areas will be significantly cheaper than gyms in urban areas.

As for figures, well, a gym membership could fall anywhere within the range of $100 per month, to $1,000 per month. Like I said before, it all depends on their location and status.

As for a budget on equipment, well it's hard to put a finger on that too since it all depends on the type of equipment you'll be buying, and whether they are brand-new or used.

Not to leave you stranded on an estimate, I'd say you should have a budget of $500 for both equipment and workout gear.

We all can't have the same budget, so you need to come up with one that suits your situation.

Chapter 2 Summary

Setting long and short term goals, and remaining disciplined towards achieving them is the only way to actualizing your bodybuilding dreams.

There will be challenges and doubts along the line, but with self-motivation, the help of your friends at the gym, patience, and consistency, you can get the kind of body you've been dreaming about.

Don't forget to draw up a budget for the expenses that come along with bodybuilding. Those protein-rich foods, supplements, gym membership, workout gear, and equipment are the things you need to help you achieve your long-term goals.

Chapter 3: How to Build Muscle Mass Effectively

Consume more calories than you burn, that is the basic rule of building muscle mass!

To build one pound of muscle, you will need to consume 2,800 calories. This can support protein turnover, and you can support muscle-growth with training.

The human body can grow a maximum of about 225g of muscle every week, so do not make the mistake of eating too many calories with hopes of building your muscles faster. That would only lead to a build-up of fat.

I'd like to start this chapter by giving you 8 proven tips on how you can build muscle mass more effectively. So keep reading!

8 Ways to Effectively Build Mass

Follow these tips, and you'll get the desired results.

1. Don't Skip Breakfast

A bodybuilder trying to build muscle mass will be making a huge mistake by skipping breakfast, as it is one of the most important meals in a day to achieving your goals.

Omelets, cottage cheese, and smoothies are examples of healthy breakfast options that will help you build muscle mass.

Kicking-off your day with a nice, healthy meal will also set the trend for other healthy meals to follow during the course of your day.

2. Eat Every 3 Hours

Yeah I know, it sounds like I'm trying to get you fat, but it's far from it. Eating small, healthy meals within this time frame will stop you from being hungry. It will also give you the calories you need to build muscle mass faster, and more effectively.

Remember, when you get hungry, there is a tendency to eat large, unhealthy, fat-filled meals, just to satisfy the intensity of your present craving. This will defeat the purpose of building muscle mass, since you're building up excess fat too (not to mention a large belly).

It is better to eat many small but healthy meals than a few large, fattening foods, as far as staying fit is concerned.

It is important to eat the right thing in this instance, or risk getting fat. Low-fat protein-filled food will be a good option here, some salmon perhaps?

3. Add Protein to Your Diet

Protein is known for being one of the best muscle-builders you can consume. To get the best results, be sure to eat at least 1g per 454g of body mass.

For a regular-sized person (who weighs around 90kg) they would need about 200g of protein on a daily basis.

To build up muscle mass effectively, you sure to add protein to all your meals, yes, ALL OF THEM!

The best way to get the desired amount of protein is to eat whole-sources of it.

Some of the best whole-sources of protein include:

- Red meat – These include beef, pork, lamb, etc.
- Poultry, such as chicken, turkey, and duck
- Fish, such as tuna, salmon, sardines, and mackerel
- Eggs (the yolk is packed with protein)
- Dairy (Milk, cheese, cottage cheese, quark, yogurt are great)
- Whey (you could make shakes after a good workout)
- Try tofu, seeds and nuts

Adding whole-source protein to your meals will do you a great deal of good, as far as building your muscles are concerned.

4. Eat Lots of Fruits and Vegetables

The good thing about fruits and vegetables is that they are low on calories, but high in fiber, which helps digestion and grows muscle mass.

Fruits are also rich in vitamins and minerals, and they are very good antioxidants.

What I love most about fruits is that you can eat them until your belly gets full, without getting fat as a whole.

5. Eat Carbohydrates after Workouts

Carbohydrates are great for boosting energy, but taking too much of it can lead to high sugar levels in the body.

However, they contain the much-needed calories for muscle growth, so you still need to consume them in good quantity, and at the right time.

The best recommended time carb consumption is right after an intensive workout.

When your workout is done, you can have some rice, bread, pasta, quinoa, potatoes, and oats.

I suggest consuming more of whole-grain carbs than white carbs.

6. Eat Healthy Fats

Healthy fats digest slowly so they are great for building muscle mass.

Steer clear of artificial trans-fats and margarine.

7. Drink Lots of Water after Training

After a rigorous training session, you will lose water through sweating, and body fluid is important to muscle recovery. Without water, your muscles will not recover fast enough.

8. Eat More of Whole Foods

Whole foods are unrefined and unprocessed. They come in pretty much their natural form, and they bring all their natural goodness along for the ride.

Whole foods are essential to muscle growth, and they are healthier to consume.

Examples of whole foods include meat, chicken, fish, rice, eggs, vegetables, quinoa, and fruits.

Processed foods usually come with unhealthy additives that add little or no value to your muscle-building cause.

Examples of processed food include ice-cream, pizza, bagels, cereals, and frozen foods.

The above-mentioned tips will give you the best results in your quest to build muscle mass.

Do I Need a Private Trainer To

Build My Muscles?

If you're a newcomer, then you probably don't know too much about building muscles. You may have tried to do it all by yourself, but the results were less than impressive.

Going to the gym is an option. There you get to meet other like-minded bodybuilders, and of course, a trained instructor. The only downside with going to the gym is that the instructor would have his/her attention divided between other bodybuilders in training.

If you want your trainer's undivided attention, then the only option here is to hire him/her privately.

This comes with one major advantage, and that's having your trainer's full attention and focus on you.

With a private trainer, you can have all your bodily details uniquely considered. Your weight, cholesterol levels, strength, resistance, tolerance etc.

With all this information made available to your private trainer, he/she can work on a training program best suited for your unique condition.

Your private trainer can also observe the progress you are making, and determine the next steps you need to take which will pull you closer to achieving your goals.

If you are not making the desired progress, your private trainer would know exactly what to do, in terms of adjusting your training programs and your diet.

All the above-mentioned advantages make it all worth it at the end of the day.

Keep in mind, however, that hiring a private trainer will cost you more than if you were training with a group, under the supervision of one trainer.

If you have a budget for this, then why not? Go ahead and hire a private trainer.

In response to the original question *"Do I need a private trainer to build my muscles?"* the answer is no, you don't necessarily need a private trainer to build your muscles.

You can train with a group and still achieve your desired results. A private trainer only adds the value of focused-training, and of course convenience.

Keep in mind also, hiring a private trainer doesn't guarantee you'll get the best results, as it is really up to you, the trainee, to be determined, focused, and consistent enough to reach your goal.

Questions You Need To Ask Yourself Before You Hire a Private Trainer

You shouldn't just hire a private trainer for the sake of it. Unless you're a celebrity or a popular personality who cherishes his privacy and doesn't want to mingle with the "regular folks".

That being said, you need to ask yourself a few questions before you hire a private trainer.

1. What am I trying to achieve?

If you are a professional bodybuilder who's prepping for a competition, then you will need the full attention of a trainer. In this case, hiring a private trainer may be a good idea, since you have a specific reason for training.

Many individual athletes have private trainers who help prepare them for tournaments or contests. Take Serena Williams for example, she has a team of private trainers who help keep her in tip-top shape.

One may work with her on fitness, while the other works with her on the technicalities of her game.

This is not the same with team sports, as every member of the team takes their training sessions together.

So, a professional bodybuilder, being an individual preparing for a competition would find it more convenient and effective if he hired a private trainer.

On the flip side, if your bodybuilding goal is just to look good and become stronger, then you don't really need a private trainer to build your muscles. You can achieve that in group-training.

2. Can I afford the services of a private trainer?

Let's assume you're not a pro bodybuilder, and you have no competition to prepare for, you might still prefer the convenience of working with a private trainer.

However, as I mentioned earlier, private trainers are more expensive to hire.

Now the question is, can you afford the expenses that come with it?

If you can, then you should go for it, if you can't, then scrap the idea.

Right personal trainers are worth their weight in gold. You may not need them every day It could be only twice per week but their periodic visits can keep you on the right track and motivated you a lot. If you do not think you are getting any benefit then try another trainer.

You don't need a guy who only says half halfheartedly "OK, just 4 more, 3 more and you are done, good job". It is a waste of money. You have to find one that shares your goals and one that you can relate to.

The trainer expertise can customize exercise plans for you. Their knowledge of recovering from specific injuries or surgeries will help prevent you from possible injuries

How much private trainer cost?

Personal training is $40 to $70 per hour session with most paying $55. For gyms such as LA Fitness or Gold's Gym, rates are $60 per hour, and group training runs $35 per class. You can get some discounts when purchasing training sessions in packages of 5, 10, or 20.

Training sessions could cost between $250 to $400 per month which includes two sessions of one hour each week. This is the price for an average trainer or at a smaller gym without all the luxury amenities of larger chains.

If you go to a more upscale gym like Equinox, expect to pay "luxury" prices of $110+ an hour. For In-Home personal training. You can actually request your personal trainer come to your home. The cost on this could be all over the place, but a rough average would be about $65 for an hour session.

But don't Think that "more expensive" means "better results." Its really depending on your goals and the results. $40 per session might be overpaying for a crap trainer who gives you a generic workout and doesn't care about you.

$110 per session can be considered as a steal if it's an amazing trainer that gets to know your life and your personality can help you only get past a plateau when you stall.

However, It's good idea to save money by booking your trainer in packages of 5, 10 or 20 sessions at a time at gym. Try to book more sessions in advance, because they are likely to give you higher the discounts.

Indeed, each trainer has a different teaching style, you choose focus of their expertise and personality. Sometimes I find female trainer can be productive because there is typically less chatting with us,

It's all about the dynamic between two people, and the styles of learning and teaching rather than the gender but If you are a large male, its not a good idea to stuck with a 110 lb female trainer. This could limit greatly in terms of your possible exercises, as many could not be done safely you're your trainer as a spotter.

When you first meet your personal trainer, talk to them about your fitness goals, workout preferences. Let's tell your trainer right away if you've had any surgery in the past, a heart condition or abnormal blood pressure.

During your first session, ask them how the exercises will progress over time. If their answers are vague, then you can tell they don't have enough experience.

However, don't expect miracles in a day. You can try to have 5 sessions before making a decision that things aren't working out, try to find sessions that are sold at a discount in a package.

Good trainers can answer you about what type of results you can expect. For example, they would say something like "You can gain 0.5 to 1 pound of muscle per week if you're bulking even when you do everything right because muscle building takes some time."

He will tell you that you can build muscle and lose fat at the same time if you're new to weightlifting or he might have conversation about bulking and cutting to beg the question of where you should start. This makes you know your would-be trainer is knowledageble enough.

3. Will I get my money's worth?

So you have a budget for a private trainer, and you're sure the extra costs won't hurt your pocket, but you still wouldn't want to waste money right?

The question that follows is whether you'll be getting your money's worth in training. Will hiring a private trainer ensure my muscles will be well built?

Not getting your money's worth may boil down to a few factors. Maybe your private trainer doesn't motivate you enough, or maybe you don't motivate yourself enough.

Value for money in this case may also boil down to the experience of the trainer you're hiring.

What is his track record? Are their client testimonies that can assure me of his competence?

Asking yourself these questions and getting the answers to them will help you determine if you'll be getting your money's worth in training.

It'll be a shame if after spending the extra bucks, you achieve poorer results than your next-door neighbor who trained in a group, and spent less money.

Best Weight Training Programs

If you are looking to add on some serious mass to your body (which I believe you are), lifting weights is a trusted means to achieving it.

Now the question is, what are the best weight training programs that will help you achieve your goal?

There are so many weight-training programs to indulge in, but I'll be looking at the very best for you!

Stay with me!

The 5X5 Program

For those who looking to build up some muscle mass and improve their strength, the 5X5 program is one you should try.

It has become very popular over the years, and for good reason too!

Here's how it works.

This program is set up to perform 3 main exercises that focus on the major muscle groups in your body. These are the lower and upper body.

You will be required to perform 5 sets 5 times.

When you finish a set, you can throw in some sets of other isolated exercises, although that is not required with this program.

Pros

The major advantage of this program is that you'll have an increased frequency of training.

This program stimulates so many muscle fibers so you will experience a significant release of testosterone. This aids in the growth of muscle mass.

Testimonies by those who have experience with this program have revealed that it actually makes them hungry.

This is a testament to how intense this program is.

Cons

This program has proven to be too intense for beginners. Their bodies just can't take it, and if they force it, they could get injured in the process.

This program is best suited for bodybuilders who have had at least a 3-month history with lifting weights.

Another downside to this program is that it's so rigorous, it may lead to fatigue, and may hinder you from engaging in other programs.

German Volume Training

The German Volume program is pretty similar to the 5X5, being that you have to do multiple sets. The difference here is that you'll have to do a much higher number of reps, 10 to be precise!

This program is designed to focus on 2 main muscle groups per day, and you alternate between them over the course of 3 days per week.

Pros

If you've had some good experience lifting weights, this program will allow you build muscle mass at an incredibly quick rate. Keep in mind that you have to follow the right nutritional protocol to do this.

If you don't pay close attention to your nutrition, your body will not be able to bear the program and you will burn out faster than you hoped for.

For best results, be sure to maintain a high-calorie diet, as this will help support the intensity of the program

Cons

Just like the 5X5 program, this one will also zap a lot of energy from you. This is not ideal if you have other workout programs to engage in.

Doing this program will mean you have to reduce other programs, just so your strength would be enough for it.

Keep in mind that your body will require adequate time to recover before you engage in any other program.

The other downside to this program is the beginner factor. If the 5X5 is not ideal for beginners, then the German volume training is completely out of it.

To qualify for this program, you must have had a minimum of one-year weight lifting experience, during which you must have built up your muscles to a reasonable extent, as well as strength and stamina. There is no other way around it.

There are modified variations of the German volume training. These advancements have seen the rep range drop, but the amount of weight increased.

You can indulge in whichever one you feel suits you the best.

The FST-7 Training Program

This is the third type of volume training program on my list, and it's getting popular pretty fast.

This program doesn't specifically state all the exercises you're required to perform in a given session, also, it does not specifically state that you must split the body up into a certain protocol (upper body and lower body or chest/back, legs and shoulder for instance).

Rather, it provides guidelines as to what you should be doing on the last exercise for each body part worked that session.

In case you're wondering what FST-7 stands for, it means Fascial Stretch Training. This indicates that one of the major goals this program tries to achieve is to stretch the fascia tissue (this is the soft connective tissue that is found around your muscles, as well as the other parts of your body).

This program requires you to perform seven sets of 15 reps for the last exercise you do for each muscle group.

For ultimate effectiveness, you are to keep your resting times between these sets pretty short, a total of 30 seconds maximum.

Pros

The advantages of this program, besides better fascia health, are that it still permits a great deal of flexibility on your part with overall structural design.

If you wish to specialize in particular body parts, you can surely do so. Also, if you'd rather keep the rest of the program lower in total volume, maybe because you don't have a quick recovery rate, you can also do that as well.

Another advantage that comes with this program is that the higher rep and set range for that one exercise will stimulate the metabolic rate significantly. So, whether your goal is muscle building or fat loss, as long as you're eating the right accompanying diet, you can see a spike in results through that manner as well.

Cons

For me, the major downside you can find with this program is, if you find it hard to recover, you may not be able to work out as frequently as you're accustomed after performing this routine.

The more you do it, the better your body gets accustomed to it. For this reason, do your best not to dump the program in a hurry.

Find enough reason to keep at it, and make sure you eat properly too!

Upper/Lower Split Training

Next on the list is the upper/lower body split. This is commonly performed on a 2 on, 1 off schedule, which lets you work on each muscle group twice in a week.

Pros

One of the advantages of this workout is that it is ideal for those who are new to bodybuilding. This is because it gives the beginner ample time to recover over the week. It also breaks the body up, meaning each rep is considerably less stressful.

Not bad for beginners looking to pile up some muscle mass.

Bodybuilders who have more experience can also use this workout to intensify their training through the total set number. Also through exercise selection and the resting period. This permits an increased level of muscle growth at any level.

There's another advantage that comes with this workout plan. It allows the trainee to include more isolated exercises in his routine. If it is your desire to improve on any of your smaller muscle groups, such as triceps, lateral deltoid, or biceps, this routine will allow you to achieve that with greater ease.

Cons

The only major issue with this program is that it is designed to be performed 4 days a week. This could be an issue if you have other engagements that would not permit you to be present at the gym.

It could be work, family functions, or your weekly visit to your psychiatrist.

The good news is, you can overcome this challenge by doing a week of lower, upper, lower training, and do upper, lower, upper training the following week.

Chapter 3 Summary

Building muscle mass takes 3 things.

- Time
- Eating the right muscle-building foods
- Doing the right exercise programs

Your muscles won't build up overnight, it will take months to start seeing significant improvements, and years before you have the body you've always dreamt of!

Chapter 4: How to Use the Gym, Fitness & Other Exercise Tools at Home

Let's face it, not every intending bodybuilder will have the time to visit the gym, especially if they have the kinds of jobs or careers that take up so much of their time.

The people who find themselves in this situation are mostly amateur bodybuilders who don't plan on making a career out of it.

Don't be discouraged, you can build your body right from the comfort of your home.

This will of course require you to buy a gym or training equipment. It will also require a high level of discipline and self-motivation to accomplish since you would most likely be training all by yourself.

Being new to the practice of bodybuilding, you may ask yourself, what are the equipment I need to train at home? You may not have an answer to that question, but I am here to help.

Keep reading, as I will soon list out the best equipment bodybuilders can use at home.

Before I do, I would like to list out some of the advantages that come with training at home.

Pros of Training at Home

Here are the major pros that come with training at home.

There are no Sign-up or registration fees: You guessed right, the owner of the gym won't just allow you to walk in and use their equipment as you please. For you to use the facilities and enjoy the privileges that come with the gym, you have to first sign-up and pay a monthly or annual registration fee.

Upon expiration of your subscription, you would be required to renew your membership, and this will also cost you some money, maybe higher than you originally paid, that's if the gym decides to increase their fees.

The reverse is the case with training at home. You won't have to register or sign-up with anyone, meaning such costs would be effectively cut out.

However, you would have to invest some money in training equipment. The good thing here is, the equipment will be yours forever, and over the years, you would find it to be cheaper than paying monthly registration fees at a gym.

Savings on transportation costs: Driving to, and back from the gym will cost you some money in gas, but that is not the case when you train at home.

Let's say you don't have a car, and you take the bus or train, that would still cost you some money. Over weeks or months, you will be alarmed to find out how much you've spent on transportation costs to the gym.

The only reasonable way you can cut out this cost is of you walk or ride a bicycle to the gym and back. This, however, would mean the gym has to be within walking or riding distance from your home. If not, you're in for a really long walk/ride.

The problem with this would be fatigue. How many sets do you think you can do after walking such a long-distance? You would be exhausted afterwards, so your guess is as good as mine.

You can create a training schedule that suits you: Gyms are not usually open 24 hours a day/7 days a week. This means you have to be at the gym during the times trainings are scheduled. These times may not fit into your personal schedule, as you may have work or other important engagements to attend to.

The privilege of training at a time that suits you is one of the biggest advantages that come with training at home.

It could be early in the morning before work, in the afternoon, or even at night. It's all up to you to choose the times that are more favorable.

No distractions: The gym could be considered a social place where several people gather, talk, and possibly become friends.

In such a situation, it is easy to get carried away by what others are doing, instead of focusing on your training.

The reverse is the case when you train at home. There will be no distractions (especially if you live alone). Even if you live with people, you would already be used to having them around so they won't be much of a bother.

Cons of Training at Home

As there are pros to training at home, there are also cons.

Some of these cons will be discussed below.

Your training may lack a professional hands-on touch: Training at home means you will most likely be without a professional trainer unless of course, you hire one. But hiring one would defeat the purpose of saving money by training at home since you will have to pay the trainer for his/her services.

That being the case, you may use YouTube videos as a guide to your training, but the problem with this is you can't interact with the trainers in YouTube videos. It would be a case of no questions asked, only instructions followed.

Not being able to ask an experienced professional some relevant questions can be a setback in your training. Also, the absence of a professional trainer would mean there will be no one to correct you when you are doing your programs wrongly.

You may become inconsistent: When you have the freedom to work out your own training schedules, you may find yourself missing sessions out of laziness. Having at the back of your mind that you won't be "scolded" by any trainer or co-trainees can put you at ease, and make you nonchalant towards your training.

On the flip side, if you were registered at a gym, your gym pals and your trainer could encourage you to keep up with training.

Even if you become lazy and miss one or two sessions, there is a high chance that one of your friends at the gym would call to check on you and ask why you've missed your sessions. Those phone calls alone can trigger you to get up and go.

Equipment maintenance: There is no piece of equipment that can't get damaged. This means if by any chance your equipment gets damaged, you will be responsible for fixing it. This doesn't come free.

On the other hand, if you were training at a gym, it would be up to the management of the gym to fix or replace any damaged equipment.

The annoying part is when your equipment gets damaged at a time you are on a tight budget. This means you won't have the money to fix it at the moment.

Such an occurrence can hinder your training, at least until you can afford to fix your equipment.

You don't have access to a wide range of equipment: Unless you live in a big house with more than enough space, and have a big budget to buy every piece of equipment you desire, then you would be stuck with what you can afford, or what can fit into the limited space you have at home.

This will not be a problem for you if you were registered at a gym. Here you will have access to a wider range of equipment, and enough space to work with them.

Equipment You Will Need To Train At Home

Many bodybuilders get skeptical when the idea of training at home pops up. Many newcomers think it's impossible, while seasoned vets know it's very achievable.

I agree with these seasoned vets who say it can be done. This is because IT CAN.

Come to think of it, as far as the training itself is concerned, the major difference between training at home and training at the gym is location.

Whatever piece of equipment you can find at the gym can also be bought and installed in your home, as long as you have the budget and space for it.

So, what equipment do you need to effectively train at home? There are 4 basic equipment you should have at your home gym.

Permit me to list them out below.

1. Adjustable dumbbells with free weight plates: Dumbbells are the first pieces of equipment you need for proper home workout.

They are also relatively inexpensive, so they should fit right into your budget.

The advantage of having adjustable dumbbells is that you can remove and stack up the weight plates as you see fit.

For a beginner, starting with the lighter weights is recommended. As the weeks go by and as your strength improves, you can gradually increase the weights on the dumbbell.

2. A bench with incline adjustments: Bodybuilding will almost be impossible without a good and sturdy bench. Bench-pressing is one of the oldest bodybuilding programs you can find and it is very effective.

Your best bet is to buy an adjustable bench, as this will allow you workout in an inclined position.

3. A chin-up bar: You can buy a chin-up bar between the $15 to $20 range. Be sure to have adequate space at home to install and use.

4. A squat-rack: This will be the largest piece of bodybuilding equipment you purchase for your home workout.

To buy a full squat-rack, you will have to have a budget of about $300, although you may end up spending as high as $400.

Squat-racks are great because they allow you perform full body workouts, although they take up a lot of space, so you'll have to dedicate a special part of your home for it.

Take precaution when you squat. Make sure you squat in an area that has adequate and secure space for you to drop the loaded bar.

If you buy a full-set squat-rack, you will find that a chin-up bar is also attached to it. This is a 2-in-1 advantage for you.

With these 5 pieces of equipment, you can start your bodybuilding journey right from the comfort of your home.

As I mentioned earlier, newcomers to the world of bodybuilding will be skeptical about the possibility of building muscles at home, but seasoned veterans and professionals know it is very possible.

As I also mentioned earlier, the only real difference between working out at the gym and working out at home, as far as the training itself is concerned, is location.

Having these 4 pieces of equipment will make your dream of training at home a reality, and you will pretty much get the same results as you would get if you had registered at the gym.

How to Use Adjustable Dumbbells

What You Will Need

Below are the things you will need before you start using adjustable dumbbells.

A set of adjustable dumbbells

The very first thing you will need are the dumbbells themselves (obviously). There are many types or brands of dumbbells to choose from, that choice is up to you to make.

Go for a set that has your preferred weight limit, as these will be ideal for you to start with. This should be a light set, since you're still in the process of building up your strength.

The more you use it, the stronger you become, hence, the more weight you can add to it as the weeks and months go by.

I recommend dumbbells of at least 50lbs each

A pair of comfortable shoes

The second thing you will need is a pair of comfortable workout shoes.

A good pair of shoes on feet will help you maintain balance as you lift. Remember, the position of your legs is vital to how effective you lift the weights.

Below are my recommended picks for weightlifting/training shoes.

- Nike Romaleo 2.0.
- Adidas Performance adiLifter
- Reebok Crossfit Lifter 2.0
- Adidas Drehkraft Shoes

The right workout clothes

Remember, lifting weights, no matter how light, will require a lot of arm and waist movement. For this reason, you have to pick out the right workout clothes for your training sessions.

The clothes you pick have to be light, and they should allow for proper breathability, since you'll be doing a lot of sweating.

Workout space

You need to dedicate an area of your home where you will have your training sessions. It could be your yard, or an empty room in your apartment, even your bedroom (if it's spacious enough).

Your workout space should be free of any obstructions on the floor. If your floor is made of tiles or hardwood, then you should have a rag or mop in hand to hand all the sweat that will drop.

If you have a rug or carpet on your floor, then you should buy a gym mat (made of plastic material). This will prevent the sweat from getting on your rug.

Music

What's a good workout without music? It will be boring!

Be sure to have a music player around. It is a known fact that music can motivate or trigger body movements, this is why you need to have some around as you train.

A workout plan to follow

Adjustable dumbbells have proven to be an important tool for bodybuilders, but you still need a workout plan to follow.

Without a proper plan, you will get less than impressive results.

Now that you have all you need for your dumbbell training sessions, I will proceed to show you some moves.

There are so many ways to use a dumbbell, you can actually invent yours (that's when you're experienced enough). However, I will be showing you the most basic moves, suitable for beginners.

Here are the steps to follow.

[Step 1] Warm-Up

To avoid having any muscle injuries, you need to do some warm-ups before you start lifting. Remember, you're a beginner, and it would be a bad idea if you just dive into it without prepping your muscles first.

Even the pros warm-up before they start!

Muscles are elastic, and just like any elastic material you know, they are stiffer when they are cold, and more flexible when they are warm.

When your muscles are flexible, they will perform better and you will have a more effective training session.

For a good warm-up, you can start off with light movements that will increase the intensity bit by bit.

If your focus for the day is working on your upper body, then that is the area you need to warm up. On the other hand, if you are planning to heat up your lower body, then that is the area the warm-up should focus on.

If you want to work on your body as a whole, then your warm-up should include your arms, legs, back, and belly areas.

[Step 2] Adjusting the Dumbbell

So, your muscles are all heated up and ready to go! Meaning it's time to get into the workout itself.

I'll be teaching you how to complete the shoulder (or deltoids), the latissimus dorsi (or the outer upper back) workout.

Here, there are 4 moves required and each step will be done with different weights. This depends on the muscles being worked.

Adjusting the weight on your dumbbell will require certain steps, but this also depends on the model of dumbbell you buy.

I will go over 3 of the most popular adjustable dumbbells in the market, and how to change the weight on each model.

1. Bowflex SelectTech Adjustable Dumbbells

This model of adjustable dumbbells come in two different sizes.

First is the 552 series, which is adjustable from 5 to 52lbs each. The second is the 1090 series, and it is adjustable from 10 to 90lbs each.

Adjusting the weight on these dumbbells is pretty straightforward. They are designed with dials on the ends, which adjust the pressure automatically.

All you have to do is turn the dial to your desired weight.

2. XMark Fitness Adjustable Dumbbells

Just like the Bowflex, these dumbbells also come in two different sizes. The first being 25lbs each and the second being 50lbs each. They are also very easy to adjust, making them perfect for beginners.

At the top of each dumbbell, there is a lever that can be slid back and forth to select the weight you want.

3. PowerBlock Adjustable Dumbbells

Unlike the first two I mentioned, these dumbbells come in 3 different sizes.

Each set comes with two dumbbells of either 50, 70, or 90lbs per hand.

Adjusting the weight on these dumbbells is a little more complicated than the first two I mentioned, but it is still relatively easy to do so.

To adjust the weight, all you are required to do is hold the pin and slide it into the slot of your desired weight.

[Step 3] First Move, the Dumbbell Shoulder Press

This is the first move we will be going through.

Here, you need to adjust your dumbbells to a weight suitable for you as a beginner. This will depend on your already existing strength, and of course your body size.

I recommend 10lbs for beginners.

With a dumbbell on each hand, raise to shoulder level, and slowly push up and down.

Complete 10 shoulder presses for a start.

[Step 4] Second Move, the Bent Over Row

The second move you need to do is the best row. You can do this with heavier weight since you'll be using your back muscles for support.

You can adjust your dumbbell weight from 10lbs to 25lbs.

To do this move, have the dumbbells in each hand, bend over slightly with your hands facing the ground and pull up and down.

Do 8-10 bent over rows for a start.

[Step 5] Third Move, the Standing Lateral Raise

This is the third move we will be looking at. This move is aimed at working on the rotator cuff.

This move doesn't put too much strain on your back, but it still requires arm-strength. This means you can reduce the weight once more. From 20lbs, you can take it down back to 10lbs.

Do 10 standing lateral raises.

[Step 6] Last Move, the Dumbbell Pullover

This is the last move in the adjustable dumbbell workout.

To do this program, you will need a few items. These include a chair, bench, or a bed. Adjust the weight of your dumbbells to about 15lbs, maybe even 10lbs. This program is pretty challenging so keep the weight light since you're a beginner.

Perform about 12 to 15 dumbbell pullovers.

So, as I have pointed out, these moves are different, and they require different weights. The good thing is, when your muscles get stronger, you can adjust the pressure on your dumbbells to see how much progress you've made strength-wise.

As the weeks pass, keep increasing the weight gradually to build strength and muscles. The desired results will follow.

Bodybuilding experts from all over the world recommend the above mentioned adjustable dumbbell programs. It has worked for thousands of people around the world, and it can work for you too!

Remember, consistency is key here, so you have to stick to your workout plan. It will also take time for you to see results, both short and long term, but it surely won't happen overnight.

Adjustable Dumbbells Vs Fixed Dumbbells

I have spoken at length about adjustable dumbbells, but haven't said anything about fixed dumbbells. Well, this is because adjustable dumbbells wins for me, and I am sure bodybuilders around the world will agree.

I will list out a few pros and cons of both adjustable and fixed dumbbells, then you can choose which is best for you.

Pros of Using Adjustable Dumbbells

Here are a few advantages that come with adjustable dumbbells.

Weight can be adjusted: This obviously is a no-brainer, as weight adjustability is what makes this dumbbell distinct from the fixed dumbbell.

The advantage of adjustability is great for beginners, who need to start off with lighter weights, then work their way up to heavier weights. With an adjustable dumbbell, you don't need to buy several dumbbells of different weights, as its weight is already adjustable.

They are relatively cheaper: Adjustable dumbbells are ideal for bodybuilders who are on a tight budget, as they are usually sold cheaper than the fixed dumbbells.

They consume less space: Since an adjustable dumbbell already caters to different weight classes, it means you won't have to buy more than a set.

This is not the case with fixed dumbbells, as you have to buy several sets that have different weights. This will obviously take up a lot more space in your room.

This is not ideal for those who live in small apartments or have limited training space.

Cons of Using Adjustable Dumbbells

Here are a few downsides to using adjustable dumbbells

Adjusting weights take time: When you want to move from one weight class to the other, you have to go through the process of adjusting the weight.

This could be time-consuming, especially when you have to move between 4 to 5 weight ranges in a single training session.

This is not the case when using fixed dumbbells. All you have to do when it's time to increase or reduce the weight is to drop the one you're holding and pick up the ones that have your desired weight.

They are not as durable as fixed dumbbells: I mentioned earlier that adjustable dumbbells are relatively cheaper than fixed dumbbells, but this still comes with a cost.

This cost comes in the form of cheaper construction materials. The cheaper the materials used in building the dumbbells, the less due they will be.

Another issue with adjustable dumbbells is that all the screwing, sliding and locking can contribute its wear-and-tear.

Pros of Using Fixed Dumbbells

Here are some of the advantages that come with using fixed dumbbells.

They are more durable: Fixed dumbbells are sturdily built and they are more durable than adjustable dumbbells.

Remember, with fixed dumbbells, there is no screwing or unscrewing, neither is there any sliding and locking required. All these movements contribute to the wear-and-tear of the dumbbells.

You can pick up an go: With fixed dumbbells, the element of adjusting weights are eliminated. There is no need to adjust the weight when you want to increase or decrease.

Just pick up and go.

There will be no time wasted adjusting weights.

Cons of Using Fixed Dumbbells

Here are a few downsides to using fixed dumbbells.

They take up too much space: With fixed dumbbells, you can't adjust the weights, this means you need to have several sets of fixed dumbbells that have different weight classes for your training sessions.

This will mean having dumbbells all over your rack and floor. This will take up too much space, and it is not ideal for people who have small spaces at their disposal.

They are more expensive: Buying many sets of fixed dumbbells can take a chunk out of your pocket, unlike adjustable dumbbells that will require you to have only one set.

If you don't have the budget for several sets of fixed dumbbells, and you're still keen on working out at home, then adjustable dumbbells would be your best bet.

Personally, i will recommend using adjustable dumbbells, especially for beginners with a limited budget, and small workout spaces.

The choice on which to use remains yours. Just be sure to go for the one that suits your needs, your budget, and your overall situation.

How to Use a Bench with Incline Adjustments

The bench press has so many variations, all of which are widely used by bodybuilding professionals and trainees all over the world. It is a program that helps build muscle mass, strength, and the overall physique of an individual.

The incline bench press can be used to build the upper pectoral muscles (the chest muscles), it is also used to improve shoulder strength and add extra muscle mass to the individual's upper body.

It is widely practiced by those in the business of powerlifting and Olympic weight lifting.

Here are a few things I'd like to discuss regarding the incline bench press program.

- Incline Bench Press Form and Technique
- Benefits of doing the Incline Bench Press
- Muscles that are worked by the Incline Bench Press
- Incline Bench Press Sets, Reps, and Weight Recommendations
- Incline Bench Press Variations and Alternatives

How to Do the Incline Bench Press-Form and Technique

The step by step form process I will discuss below is with regards to the incline bench press using a barbell.

You wouldn't find these steps strange if you are already used to working the dumbbells, or the specialty bar. This is not to say that there are no slight differences in the process because there are.

Follow these steps!

Step 1: Set a bench so that the incline is roughly 15-30 degrees vertical within a power rack

When the incline of the bench is raised to a greater height, the dependency on your shoulder will increase.

Step 2: Set the hips and upper back on the bench, with the feet strongly rooted into the floor

In this bench press position, lifters will be enabled to brace harder, as well as stabilize loads.

Step 3: There may be a variation in grip width, nonetheless, the width of the hands should be a bit wider than the width of the shoulders.

Here's a quick tip, at the bottom of the bench press, be sure to position the forearms perpendicular to the ground.

If the grip width is too wide or too narrow, it would result in the forearms angling outwards/inwards.

Step 4: Unrack the barbell so that the bar is stabilized above the upper chest/shoulders.

To stabilize this position, forcefully retract the shoulder blades and squeeze the barbell.

Step 5: Pull the barbell to the chest, being sure to actively use the back muscles to keep the chest and shoulders from rounding forwards

As the bar is lowered, the lifter should actively stretch the pectoral muscles, making sure to keep the shoulder back on the bench.

Step 6: While keeping the elbows pulling inwards towards the body, press the bar upwards and extend the elbows

Make sure you maintain control and stability during this phase. Also, make sure that your elbows do not flare out, and your shoulders must remain back on the bench.

Incline Bench Press-Muscles Worked

The incline bench press targets the muscles listed below.

Pectorals (Chest)

The major muscles that are worked during the inclined bench press are the chest muscles.

Generally, any bench press targets the chest muscles, but the inclined bench press gives the chest muscles more work to do, since the bench is inclined, and the user's body is tilted to an increased angle.

(more vertical, typically 15-30 degrees from horizontal).

Anterior Deltoids

The anterior deltoid (shoulder) is very active when doing the inclined bench press program.

When the lifter takes up a more vertical pressing plane, they will start to target the anterior deltoids and the upper chest.

If the trainee were to press in a completely vertical overhead fashion, most of the movement would be targeted towards the deltoids as a whole.

Triceps

By doing an incline bench press program, the triceps are worked in a similar fashion as the flat bench press.

Benefits of the Incline Bench Press

Below are the major benefits of doing the inclined bench press.

- Stimulate Upper Body Muscle Gain
- Isolate the Upper Pecs (Chest)
- Increase Both Pressing and Overhead Strength

Who Should Do the Inclined Bench Press?

Strongman Athletes and Powerlifters: Upper body mass and strength cannot be built without arduous training programs. The inclined bench press helps lifters bridge the gap between the flat bench press, and train all pressing movements across the most common angles you can find in sport.

Also, doing the inclined bench press will build the upper pectorals, triceps, and shoulders in a way that is quite different from the flat bench press. This helps stimulate new muscle hypertrophy and strength gains.

Olympic Weightlifters and Competitive Fitness Athletes

Similar to other pressing movements (overhead press, dips, and flat bench press), the incline bench press is another form of pressing movement which can be used to increase overall upper-body pressing strength, muscle mass, and rectify any weaknesses power-lifters may have due to lack of size or strength in the chest, shoulders, and triceps

Both weightlifting and competitive fitness require that the chest, triceps, and shoulders should create high amounts of force to accelerate loads overhead, stabilize loads overhead, and create force during front rack positions and gymnastic movements.

General Health and Wellness

Improving upper body strength, and muscle mass in general is beneficial for many bodybuilders in most movements of fitness and everyday lift.

The inclined bench press is mainly used to improve upper body strength and hypertrophy and progress towards a more functional, open-chained, and dynamic movement.

Inclined Bench Press Sets, Reps, and Weight Recommendations

Below, I will be laying out some recommendations for the inclined bench press sets, and the ideal weight suggestions, especially for beginners.

Listed below, are 4 sets, reps, and weight (intensity) recommendations for coaches and athletes to properly program the incline bench press, specific to the individual's training goal.

Please keep in mind, that the guidelines listed below are only here to provide coaches and athletes tested recommendations for programming.

Movement Integrity – Reps, Sets, and Weight Recommendations

Similar to most exercises, it is advised that the incline bench press should be done first with moderate to light loads. This will help with controlled repetitions. Doing this will also acquaint a lifter for the overall loading stress.

- 3-4 sets of 8-10 repetitions with light to moderate loads, at a controlled speed (focusing on proper eccentric/lowering of the weight), resting as needed

Muscle Hypertrophy – Reps, Sets, and Weight Recommendations

You can do the inclined bench press using both heavy and moderate loads for a blend of low to moderate volume work sets with moderate rests.

- 3-5 sets of 6-12 repetitions with moderate to heavy loads or 2-4 sets of 12-15 repetitions with moderate loads to near failure, keeping rest periods between 45-90 seconds

Strength – Reps, Sets, and Weight Recommendations

The incline bench press can be done in pretty much the same format as other strength lifts, with coaches and athletes using moderate to heavy loads for low to moderate rep ranges with longer rests. The recommendations below may be used as a basic guideline for developing greater pressing strength, using the incline bench press.

- 3-5 sets of 4-6 repetitions, with moderate to heavy loading, resting as required

Muscle Endurance- Reps, Sets, and Weight Recommendations

The recommended below sets, repetition, loading, and resting period may be used to improve muscle endurance and/or muscle hypertrophy (due to decreased rest periods and high volume).

- 2-4 sets of 15-20 repetitions with light to moderate loads, maintain a resting period of under 30-45 seconds

Inclined Bench Press Variations

Below are 3 incline bench press variations which coaches and athletes can use to substitute the standard, incline barbell bench press.

1. Incline Dumbbell Bench Press

The dumbbell incline bench press is quite the same as the incline bench press, however, it has major benefits, which includes maximizing muscle growth.

For some lifters, the position of the barbell and the various positions of the shoulder may cause pain or discomfort in the press, which will limit the amount of muscle loading, and the lifter's ability to train.

By using dumbbells, a lifter can manipulate the angle of the weights, wrist, elbows, and shoulder joint to cater to any stress/pain/or shoulder flare-ups.

The dumbbell incline press is a unilateral exercise, this means it can be done to address movement asymmetries and muscle imbalances which could negatively impact the lifter's shoulder health, chest development, and pressing ability.

2. Single Arm Incline Dumbbell Bench Press

Similar to the double dumbbell incline bench press, the single dumbbell variation can increase the lifters need to support and stabilize a load-in unilaterally.

When making use of one dumbbell, the lifter must control and resist spinal rotations and other rotational forces to the body. Also, some lifters find that they can actually concentrate on contracting the muscle as hard as they can when training single-hand pressing.

3. Tempo Incline Bench Press

Tempo repetitions have the ability to increase time under tension, enhance motor recruitment, and force trainees to slow down to better load the muscles and save the joints.

How to Use a Chin-up Bar

The pull-up exercise is one of the most overlooked exercises for building upper body, back, and core strength.

It requires a chin-up bar, which can be freestanding or you can purchase a simple doorway bar.

The traditional pull-up uses an overhand grip on the bar, while the chin-up is a variation that generally uses an underhand grip.

If you are new to pull-ups, there are many modified versions that can be used to build the strength needed to perform them.

Pull-ups can be part of an upper-body strength workout or a circuit training workout.

Benefits

The pull-up mainly targets the latissimus dorsi (lats) which is the large back muscle at the back of your arms, but it also works most of your chest, upper back, and shoulder muscles. Your abs are involved in stabilizing you as well. Strengthening your upper body will help you with your everyday tasks and maintain good posture.

Step-by-step Instructions

The pull-up bar should be at a height that requires you to jump up to grab it, and your feet should hang free. Stand below the bar with your feet apart. Jump up and grab the bar with an overhand grip. Fully extend your arms so you are in a dead hang. Bend your knees and cross your ankles for a balanced position.

Exhale while pulling yourself up so your chin is level with the bar. Pause at the top.

Lower yourself (inhaling as you go down) until your elbows are straight.

Repeat the movement without touching the floor.

Complete the number of repetitions your workout requires.

Common Mistakes

Avoid these mistakes so you can get the best out of your pull-ups and prevent injuries.

Too Fast or Sloppy

The entire movement should be slow and controlled. Once your form deteriorates, it's time to stop and take a rest or you may risk injury.

Wide Grip

If your grip is too wide you won't be able to have the full range of motion.

Short Range of Motion

You will get the best out of doing a full extension of the arms at the bottom and bringing your chin to bar level at the top. If you have gained enough strength for this full range of motion, don't cheat yourself, just do partial raises.

Wrists and Thumbs

Your wrists should not be flexed. they should remain in a neutral position throughout the pull-up. Your thumb should be on the same side of the bar as your fingers, not wrapped around it.

Flared Elbows

Your elbows are kept close to your body throughout the pull-up. Do not let them be flared out.

Kipping

Kipping is using lower body momentum to perform the pull-up. It is used in some forms of workouts but it is not considered to be proper for a strict pull-up. It should not be used unless you have perfected your pull-up form and you have been coached on how to use kipping in a controlled manner.

Modifications and Variations

Need a Modification?

If you can't do one full pull-up yet, there are several ways to develop your strength so you can start doing pull-ups.

Pull-up assist machine: Start by using a pull-up assist machine. You'll have to go to a gym for this, but it's a good way to begin building the strength needed for the pull-up.

Human assistance: You can hire a trainer, coach, or spotter to help you. Keep your knees bent and ankles crossed. Your partner will provide a gentle lift while gripping the tops of your feet. This form of assist helps offset your weight as you pull up.

Static pull-ups: Use a box or step to lift yourself into the pull-up "finish" position, and hold your chin at bar level for as long as you can. This will build your upper body strength over time. Slowly move into the negative pull-up exercise (see below) over several weeks.

Negative pull-ups: Use a box or step to lift yourself into the pull-up "finish" position, and hold your chin at bar level for several seconds. Slowly lower yourself in a controlled motion, stopping and holding at several points along the way. When you get to the bottom, repeat the process.

Half pull-ups: Stand on a box or bench that allows your elbows to bend about 90 degrees as you grip the bar. Starting your pull-up from this position requires far less strength than starting with fully extended elbows. Finish a few pull-ups this way first, then lower the box and straighten your elbows over time for a tougher pull-up.

Jumping pull-ups: Stand on a box or bench that allows your elbows to bend slightly as you grip the bar. Bend your knees until your elbows are fully extended, then "jump" up to the pull-up "finish" position with your chin level with the bar. Slowly lower yourself back to the box and repeat. Over time, you will build strength until you can attempt other pull-up variations.

Lat pull-down: The lat pull-down machine is another way to begin building the strength needed for the pull-up. With this machine, you stay seated with your knees held down and you pull the weight down to you. It's an entirely different body position and angle, but it's a fairly safe way to get started.

Extra Challenge?

If you can perform perfect pull-ups, add a challenge by attaching a weight to a weight belt while doing them or perform them while wearing a weighted vest.

Safety and Precautions

Do not attempt this exercise if you have a back, neck, shoulder, elbow, or wrist injury. Talk to your doctor or trainer about what is appropriate. The heavier you weigh, the tougher it will be for you to do pull-ups.

It is best to limit doing pull-ups to just two days each week to avoid strains and injuries. Allow at least one day off from pull-ups between sessions. When using a bar, be sure it is secure and stable in order to prevent accidental falls.

How to Use a Squat Rack

Squats are one of the most important exercises you can perform in your quest to build strong legs and stamina.

Being one of your toughest lifts, they are very vital in building strength and muscle mass. So if you're looking to workout at home, then buying a squat rack is going to be one of the best decisions you ever made, training-wise.

For the sake of working on your squats, you can get a full-body workout with just a rack, bench and a few weights.

They are heavy-duty, versatile, and ideal for working on several muscle groups all at the same time. So, not only are you getting all your compound exercises in, but you're also getting more out of the time you spend training.

Having a rack is particularly important for being able to train safely. Not only do they allow you to get a loaded bar safely onto your shoulders, but they'll stop the bar from falling on you if you fail or drop the bar, both of which are important for being able to perform squats safely.

But as you start training with a squat rack more frequently, you'll realize they can help with so many various types of exercises. And the more you mix it up with your standard exercises, the stronger you'll become. Because by working the same muscles regularly in a variety of ways, you maintain the need for your body to grow and adapt, which is the key to getting stronger.

Below we go through our full-body workout using our Adjustable Weight Bench and Squat Rack Kit.

We're mainly using a barbell but there are a few variants you can do with dumbbells too, which are really important for keeping a check on any imbalances you have going on in your body.

And as you start to build out your home gym, you can start working on some specialty bars too such as an EZ Curl Bar or a Swiss Bar – which are both great for easing any strain on your wrists and shoulders.

Full Body Squat Rack Workout

Squat racks in general will give you a really good workout. However, an adjustable squat rack is going to give you so many more options, which can be handy when you're working out at home or just have a limited amount of space.

And because this set comes with an adjustable weight bench as well, there are even more options. So, you can include variants such as incline and decline bench presses, as well as reverse flyes and weight bench lateral flyes.

We've picked out our favorite exercises that will give you will help you build strength as well as give you an all-round workout.

Exercise You Can Do With a Squat Rack

Back Squats

These are basically classic squats where the barbell is positioned at the bottom of your shoulders. This puts the weight directly over your posterior chain. They are great for working your quads, as well as your hamstrings, glutes, core and lower back.

Expert tip: keep your toes pointed out slightly with your feet a little wider than hip-width apart. Doing this will help you increase the depth of your squat.

Flat Bench Press

Great for targeting both your pecs and your triceps, flat bench presses will give you the weight you need to build muscle and get stronger. Set the spotter bars so they are just above your chest and make sure the bar rests are low enough for you to comfortably unrack the bar to get started.

Expert tip: the bar path for doing bench presses isn't straight. If you imagine watching the bar from the side, it should go from above your eye-line, down to the bottom of your chest.

Another point to remember when doing bench presses is to keep your elbows tucked in slightly. Pushing your shoulders too far back can put you at risk of injury.

Should Press

Weight benches are designed to support you while you train, helping you to keep your posture and guide your movements. By doing shoulder presses on a weight bench, your upper body needs to work harder, because you haven't got the extra push and momentum you would normally get from doing them standing up.

Expert tip: bring the barbell down to around ear height before pushing back up. Remember not to lock your elbows when you reach the top of the exercise.

Barbell Lunges

Lunges don't require a high level of hip flexibility to be able to get to full depth, which makes them great for doing more intense levels of glute, hamstring and quad work. As well as doing standard lunges, you can also use the weight bench to do Bulgarian split squats which are great for building strength as well as giving you a challenging workout.

Expert tip: lunges don't just work one leg, they work both. However, the muscles worked in each leg are slightly different depending on which one is in front and which one is behind. Practice lunging with just the barbell at first to make sure you get a feel for doing them with a weight bar. Remember to engage your core to help keep you steady.

Bicep Curls

One of the best and most simple exercises you can do to build your arms. By using a barbell, you can take on a larger amount of weight so these are great for building muscle mass.

Expert tip: you can vary your bicep curls by going just from full extension to half extension, then back down; then from half extension to full contraction, back to halfway.

Dips

Your adjustable squat rack kit can be slid all the way in to form a dip station. Dips are great for working your chest, arms and core, as well as your wrists and forearms.

Expert tip: vary your dip stance to target both your chest and your triceps, to get a great upper body workout.

Hip Lifts

Hip lifts are one of the best ways to target your glutes, as well as your hamstrings and lower back. You want to sit with the weight bench behind you so the edge is near the middle of your back. Bring your knees in and then squeeze your glutes as you lift up.

Expert tip: Use a Barbell Squat Pad to help protect your hips while using a loaded bar.

Barbell Rows

Barbell rows are a great way to work your upper back and you can vary your grip to help focus either your biceps or triceps.

Expert tip: start with the bar on the spotters and squat down so that your back is as close to parallel to the floor while keeping your spine straight. Then row the bar towards the bottom half of your abs, squeezing your shoulders together before releasing back down.

You can also do this exercise using a pair of dumbbells which will help break down any asymmetries.

Box Squats

Box squats are a great way to build up strength in your posterior chain. They also help you push your weight back so you can gradually improve your squat form.

Expert tip: bring the weight bench into the squat rack space and have it completely flat to make sure it stays balanced. Squat down and use the bench for support but don't let your back flex or relax, you want to maintain your form the whole time. Pause and then slowly push back up to start again.

How Often Should I Increase Weights on Squats

Weight load depends on how new you are to training, your current ability and what your goals are.

Essentially, to get stronger, you want to gradually keep increasing the weight load by working through the build/endurance cycle for each level.

This is a case of taking it up a notch to the point where you can do around five reps max. Then keep increasing the reps until you can do around 12 reps with the same weight load. Then take it up again and continue training back at five rep max.

What Determines How Often We Can Train (When Bodybuilding)

Years ago, before research into muscle growth reached into the fitness industry, people looked to high-profile bodybuilders to learn how often they should train a muscle group. In all fairness, most people training to improve their physique probably still do!

Anyway, at that time, a popular approach was to train each muscle group once per week. These days, since research is showing that higher training frequencies lead to greater gains in muscle size over the same period of time, bodybuilding coaches are tending to build training programs that work muscle groups twice or even three times per week.

I'm not going to talk about optimal training frequency since that will require an article of its own. Neither am I going to discuss what determines how often you can do strength training workouts as an athlete, because in the large majority of cases that is determined predominantly by fitting training around sports practices.

Rather, I am going to explain what determines how often you can train when bodybuilding, which is how fast you can recover from the muscle damage caused by the last workout involving the same muscle group.

What Determines Training Frequency?

When talking about training frequency, there are two things to consider.

Firstly, there is the change in muscle protein synthesis (MPS) rate that occurs after the workout. The increase in MPS rate is what adds protein to the muscle, which makes it larger. There is little point in doing another workout while MPS rate is still elevated since the stimulus is (probably) not additive. Therefore, we want to be doing our next workout for the same workout once MPS rates have largely returned to resting levels.

Secondly, there is the muscle-damaging effect of the workout.

MPS Rate

Once a workout is completed, MPS rate increases above resting levels for approximately 24–36 hours in trained individuals. The shape of the curve involves a large spike to 150% above resting levels in the first 12 hours, followed by a fairly long tail at ~25% above resting levels thereafter.

While some training variables (like higher volumes) can increase the size of the response in MPS rate after a workout, they probably do not have a substantial effect on the duration over which the rate is elevated.

In other words, regardless of the type workout that is completed, the effects of increased MPS rate on increasing muscle size are probably complete within 36 hours, and a large proportion of their effects likely occur within 12 hours.

In practical terms, most bodybuilders considering increasing their training frequency are thinking about shifting from training a muscle group 1–2 times per week to 2–3 times per week. Even training three times per week would involve taking 48 hours between workouts, which is longer than the 36 hours over which MPS rate is elevated.

So unless we want to train the same muscle group daily, we probably don't need to think about the transient elevations in MPS rates that carefully.

Muscle Damage

Muscle damage is caused by the internal stresses within the muscle.

Now, we normally tend to think of muscle fibers as acting independently of one another, like a bundle of strings that never touch one another. Yet, they are actually linked to each other by lateral attachments and grouped into bundles by collagen wrappings. These bundles are contained within an outer wrapping of collagen that restricts the whole muscle to a constant volume, irrespective of the behavior of the individual muscle fibers.

These links and wrappings mean that individual muscle fibers are constantly experiencing all kinds of different internal stresses in all directions when a muscle is lengthened or shortened, whether actively or passively.

Ultimately, muscle fibers are damaged when these internal stresses applied to them are too large for them to withstand while lengthening, such that they are required to absorb too much energy.

The amount of energy that a muscle fiber must absorb while lengthening is determined by the type and magnitude of the mechanical loading applied, while the amount of energy that a muscle fiber can absorb at any given time is determined by its state of fatigue. Thus, factors that affect mechanical loading and factors that affect fatigue can both influence the amount of muscle damage that is caused.

Moreover, muscle fibers experience progressively greater amounts of muscle damage over multiple reps and sets as they are damaged and become weaker (i.e. the amount of energy they can absorb is reduced), such that the amount of muscle damage increases over a workout.

Importantly, muscle damage can vary hugely, both between individuals and between workouts. And while each trainee needs to determine their own recovery rate from each type of workout, there are some types of training that cause more muscle damage than others.

What determines how much muscle damage is caused by a workout? 1st Part

Strength training workouts can be constructed in many different ways, by varying the training variables. Common training variables include:

- Contraction mode (eccentric, concentric, isometric, or stretch-shortening cycle)
- Relative load (percentage of one repetition-maximum)
- External load type (constant load or accommodating resistance)
- Range of motion
- Exercise selection
- Volume
- Proximity to failure
- Rest period duration
- Repetition duration (tempo)

Each of these training variables influences the magnitude of the muscle growth that results from a workout, probably by directly increasing the rate of muscle protein synthesis (MPS) by a slightly different amount. Each training variable also affects the amount of muscle damage that is produced.

Many of the above training variables affect mechanical loading while the muscle is lengthening (contraction mode, relative load, external load type, range of motion, exercise selection, and volume), while others influence the degree of fatigue (volume, proximity to failure, rest period duration, and tempo).

In many cases, those training variables that increase muscle damage also enhance muscle growth (volume is a good example). In such cases, muscle damage is impossible to avoid. Yet, in other cases, a great deal of muscle damage is produced by a training variable, while muscle growth is not increased substantially.

By selecting training variables that minimize muscle damage but which do not also reduce muscle growth, we can increase the rate of strength recovery after a workout, and thereby train more frequently.

What determines how much muscle damage is caused by a workout? — 2nd Part

Clearly, exercise selection plays a key role in whether muscle damage is caused, both because of the biomechanics of the exercise (which determines the nature of the internal stresses within the muscle) and because of the novelty of the exercise to the individual (which determines whether the muscle fibers have ever experienced those types of internal stresses previously).

Yet, exercise selection needs to be considered on a muscle-by-muscle basis, and I don't have space for that here.

Conversely, while longer ranges of motion (ROM) produce more muscle damage than shorter ones, full ROMs do not always cause more muscle growth than partial ones. Partial ROMs probably win out when the muscle has a very long internal moment arm length (leverage) in the middle of the exercise ROM, because this forces the full ROM to use a load that is too small to keep tension on the muscle at all times.

Thus, ROM also needs to be considered on a muscle-by-muscle basis.

However, there are two training variables that always affect mechanical loading while the muscle is lengthening (contraction mode and external load type) and two that always affect fatigue/time under tension (rest period duration and tempo), which increase muscle damage when they are used to make a workout harder, but which probably do not provide any incremental benefit for muscle growth.

1. Contraction mode (eccentric, concentric, isometric, and stretch-shortening cycle)

Eccentric-only training (using only the lowering phase of an exercise) has historically been believed to produce more muscle growth than concentric-only (using only the lifting phase of an exercise).

Yet, new research indicates that muscle growth is probably comparable between eccentric-only and concentric-only training, albeit that eccentrics cause more growth longitudinally, while concentrics cause more growth transversely. In fact, rodent model research indicates that muscle growth is comparable regardless of whatever contraction type is used when mechanical loading is fixed at the same level.

Importantly, eccentric-only training involves far more muscle damage than other types of training. Similarly, stretch-shortening cycle exercise, which involves an eccentric phase, produces more muscle damage than an isometric contraction, so long as the isometric is not performed in a stretched position.

To maximize muscle growth while minimizing muscle damage, reducing the exposure to eccentric contractions will help. This can be done by incorporating concentric-only lifts, reducing the load in the eccentric phase (use a spotter to help), or incorporating isometrics at short or moderate muscle lengths.

2. External load type (constant load and accommodating resistance)

When we lift a weight, we are using a constant load. The weight on the bar does not change over the exercise range of motion (ROM). However, the system force does change, because we are lifting against the effects of both gravity and inertia. Gravity remains the same over the exercise ROM, but inertia increases force at the beginning and reduces it towards the end.

In many popular free-weight exercises (such as the squat), this means that lifting weights involves peak mechanical loading at a long muscle length. In contrast, using accommodating resistance by adding bands and chains to a lighter barbell weight involves peak mechanical loading at more moderate muscle lengths.

The stronger contraction at longer muscle lengths caused by free weights will likely increase muscle damage, but does not appear to have a beneficial effect on the resulting muscle growth, which is similar between training with constant loads and accommodating resistance.

To maximize muscle growth while minimizing muscle damage, use accommodating resistance whenever an exercise feels hardest at the bottom of the lifting phase (where the muscle is lengthened).

3. Fatigue and time under tension (rest period duration and tempo)

Although muscle damage is most commonly discussed in the context of high forces during lengthening contractions, fatigue and time under tension are contributory factors.

Indeed, when isometric contractions are performed for long durations, this causes meaningful muscle damage, which has been attributed to the build-up calcium and neutrophils (inflammatory agents), which may degrade the inside of the muscle cell, causing damage.

Similarly, very short rest periods (less than 1 minute) also produce more muscle damage than more moderate rest periods, both in humans and in animal models (where muscle activation is maximal, indicating that the degree of motor unit recruitment is not the driving factor).

Even so, neither repetition duration (tempo) nor rest period duration have a beneficial effect on muscle growth, with the caveat that slow tempos in the eccentric phase do cause greater hypertrophy. However, this occurs because slowing down the rate of lowering a weight increases the force, because it involves resisting gravity more, and we probably want to move away from focusing on the eccentric phase if our goal is increasing training frequency.

To maximize muscle growth while minimizing muscle damage, we can use moderately long rest periods, and avoid deliberately slow tempos (self-selected movement speeds are likely best). In practical terms, increasing training frequency probably involves training multiple body parts on the same day, so supersets are a good choice to make use of the longer rests between sets of the same muscle group.

Food For Thought

As a bodybuilder, increasing training frequency involves minimizing muscle damage within a workout, while maintaining a high stimulus for muscle growth. Selecting training variables that minimize muscle damage, but which do not also reduce muscle growth, will increase the rate of strength recovery after a workout, and thereby allow you to train more frequently.

Eccentric contractions, constant loads, very short rest periods, and slow tempos increase muscle damage when they are used to make a workout harder, but probably do not provide any incremental benefit for muscle growth.

To increase training frequency, employ more concentric-only contractions (use a spotter to help), isometrics at short or moderate muscle lengths, longer rest periods (use supersets), and avoid slow tempos (self-selected speed is fine). Smart exercise selection (and the corresponding range of motion) is also valuable, but needs to be considered on a muscle-by-muscle basis.

Chapter 4 Summary

It is very possible to train and build your body right in the comfort of your home. All you will need is the right equipment, as well as the right training plan.

If you have the budget for it you can hire a personal trainer, although that would cost you more. The more budget-friendly option is to train all by yourself, with the help of books like this one, or video tutorials.

Chapter 5: Proven Models That Successful Bodybuilders Use

For those looking to transform their bodies to a well-carved structure, and wonder how the pros do it, then keep reading, as we will be looking into the training program, bodybuilding workout routines, and the type of diet it will take to transform you to a pro bodybuilder physique.

These models have been used by pro bodybuilders all over the world. It worked for them and it will work for you!

I have to mention that if you aren't already in decent shape and already training, this pro bodybuilder model will be of little use to you.

You must already have a very decent amount of lean muscle mass and have decent conditioning to follow these models for best results.

This guide is going to cater to mostly the following:

- Those who have been training regularly for a good number of years
- Those who have put on a reasonable and consistent amount of lean muscle mass for the past 3 years
- Those who have at the minimum, 10 to 12 percent body fat
- Those who have the time and discipline for a rigorous nutrition and workout schedule

Now that we are clear on the requirements, let's get into the models pro bodybuilder's use to attain the ultimate physique.

Pro Bodybuilder Physique

Training Program Weeks 1-6

All through weeks 1 to 6, the major focus should be increasing your strength and lean muscle mass gains.

This is the period where you want to emphasize gaining as much hard lean muscle mass as you can before you start the other stages of dieting and conditioning.

This implies that for 6 weeks, you must emphasize 3 major training principles:

- Heavy Compound Exercise Movements
- Eccentric Emphasis
- Continuous Overload

Compound exercises will work your body's biggest and strongest muscle groups and permit you to gain more lean muscle mass than emphasizing the smaller shaper exercises.

Merging the most effective muscle gaining compound exercises with eccentric emphasis gives you the best of the two, this is because the eccentric portion of the repetition (lowering the weight each rep), breaks down more lean muscle mass and creates more micro-tears than the concentric portion of the repetition.

Continuous overload means that each week, you must aim to increase the weight by a small percentage, so your body is forced to adapt to the extra weight and gain more lean muscle tissue.

Pros recommend adding a minimum of 5 lbs to each of the compound exercises every week.

They also recommend a 5-day split, breaking up the muscle groups using the most effective exercises for each one.

Mondays

Exercises: Barbell bench press, Db Incline bench Press, barbell incline bench press, Db flat bench press, weighted dips

Total Sets: 5

Repetition Range: 6-8

Rest Time: 2 Minutes

Focus: Eccentric Emphasis (3 Seconds on the Way Down)

Tuesdays

Exercises: Barbell Squat, Db Walking Lunges, Leg Press Machine, Hack Squat, Standing Barbell Curl, And Heavy Db Hammer Curl

Total Sets: 5

Repetition range: 6-8

Focus: Eccentric Emphasis

Wednesdays

Exercises: Stiff Leg Dead Lift, Hamstring Leg Curl Machine, Single-Leg Hamstring Curl, Ez Bar Skull Crush (Decline), Db Overhead Triceps, Weighted Dips(triceps variation)

Total Sets: 5

Repetition Range: 6-8

Rest Time: 2 Minutes

Focus: Eccentric Emphasis

Thursday

Exercises: Weighted Wide Grip Pull-Ups, Seated Row, Db 1 arm row, Barbell Row, Weighted Close Grip Pull-Ups

Total Sets: 5

Rep Range: 6-8

Rest Time: 2 Minutes

Focus: Eccentric Emphasis

Friday

Exercises: Db Shoulder Press, Seated Military Press, Barbell Shrug, Db Shrugs, Db Arnold Press

Total Sets: 5

Rep Range: 6-8

Rest Time: 2 Minutes

Focus: Eccentric Emphasis

Saturday and Sundays (Rest Days)

Phew! What a week right?

Be sure to kick back, relax, and enjoy the days you have off. Pros also recommend that you restrain from drinking alcohol, as well as other stressful activities during your resting days, as this will spike your cortisol levels and will be counterproductive to building lean muscle mass.

Training Program Weeks 7-12

The single major difference in training in weeks 7-12 is that you are only required to do 3 sets of the heavy eccentric emphasis compound exercises done from weeks 1-6.

You are also going to infuse high repetition shapers to improve your high levels through lactic acid training.

This will be vital to shaping your ultimate bodybuilder physique and attain the conditioning required for pro competitions.

This particular work-out strategy is very effective because you will be getting the best of the two. This is so because you will be lifting heavy weights and retaining your lean mass while performing high repetition shapers, and burning more body fat in specific areas of your body.

You are also going to reduce the resting period in the middle of sets, for the sake of getting in extra cardio workouts during weeks 7 through 12.

You are required to rest for about 60 seconds between compound exercises, and 30 seconds between shaper lifts.

Mondays

Exercises: Barbell Bench Press, Db Incline Bench Press, Barbell Incline Bench Press, Db flat Bench press, Weighted Dips

Total Sets: 3

Repetition Range: 6-8

Focus: Eccentric Emphasis (3 Seconds on the Way Down)

Fat Burning Shapers: Low Cable Fly Machine, Pec Fly Machine, Weighted Pushups

Total Sets: 3

Rep Range: 15-20

Kai Greene Bodybuilding Workout Routines

Famous American IFBB pro bodybuilder, Kai Green's workout routine is outlined below.

Tuesdays

Exercises: Barbell Squat, Db Walking Lunges, Leg Press Machine, Hack Squat, Standing Barbell Curl, And Heavy Db Hammer Curls

Total Sets: 3

Repetition Range: 6-8

Focus: Eccentric Emphasis

Fat Burning Shapers: Leg Extension, Db Palms Up Curl, Double Bicep Cable Curl

Rep Range: 15-20

Wednesdays

Exercises: Stiff Leg Dead Lift, Hamstring Leg Curl Machine, Single-Leg Hamstring Curl, Ez Bar Skull Crush (Decline), Db Overhead Triceps, Weighted Dips(triceps variation)

Total Sets: 3

Repetition Range: 6-8

Focus: Eccentric Emphasis

Fat Burning Shapers: Hamstring Ball Curl, Rope Triceps Extension, And Underhand Grip Triceps Extension

Thursday: Back Day

Exercises: Weighted Wide Grip Pull-Ups, Seated Row, Db 1 arm row, Barbell Row, Weighted Close Grip Pull-Ups

Total Sets: 3

Rep Range: 6-8

Focus: Eccentric Emphasis

Fat Burning Shapers: Underhand Grip Lat Pulldown, Assisted Machine Regular Pull-Ups, Isometric Pull Up Hold

Friday

Exercises: Db Shoulder Press, Seated Military Press, Barbell Shrug, Db Shrugs, Db Arnold Press

Total Sets: 3

Rep Range: 6-8

Fat Burning Shapers: Rear Delt Fly, Db Shoulder Shapers, Single-Arm Lat Raise, Db seated shrugs

Total Sets: 3

Rep Range: 15-20

Saturday and Sunday: Rest Days

The resting days you have become more important in weeks 7 through 12, as you prepare to put the final touches to your desired bodybuilder physique.

Be sure to get adequate rest and maintain the required diet on your resting days to reap the benefits of all the work you've put in the gym.

Diet Strategy Weeks 1-12

The diet strategy will remain regular for 12 weeks on this plan. You want to make the best of your post-workout window of opportunity to gain lean muscle mass through well-planned insulin spiking and carbohydrate loading.

At every other time of the day, you should have periods of low insulin, this will result to a maximum loss of fat. You can accomplish this with meals made up of lean proteins and healthy fats.

You should also consume a lot more carbohydrates on workout days as against non-workout days.

Looking at the sample meal plan below. Let's say you are training 5 days per week, you will have to stick to the workout meal plan for 5 days, and the non-workout meal plan for 2 days.

This will increase your ability to gain and retain all of your lean muscle mass tissue, while slowly shedding body fat each week.

Going by this meal plan you should be able to maintain gains and lose 0.5-1.0 lbs of body fat each week.

If you kicked off the 12-week bodybuilder prep with 10% body fat, this will allow you to get to bodybuilder level of conditioning by week 12(around 5 percent).

Protein:

Workout and Non Workout Days: 1.25 Grams per lb of bodyweight

Carbohydrates:

(Workout Days): 1.50 Grams per lb of bodyweight

(Non-Workout Days): 0.25 grams per lb of bodyweight)

Fat:

(Workout Days): .25 grams per lb of bodyweight

(Non-Workout Days): .40 grams per lb of bodyweight

Meal Plan Sample

(Workout Days)

Breakfast:

- 6 Egg Whites with 2 Whole Eggs
- ¾ Cup Whole Grain Rolled Oats
- 1 Banana

Snack 1:

- Whey Isolate Protein Shake
- 1 Ounce Mixed Nuts

Lunch:

- 10 Ounces Grilled Chicken Breast
- ½ Cup Brown Rice
- 1 Cup Steamed Veggies

Snack 2:

- 6 Ounces Fish, ½ Avocado

Post Workout Meal:

- 8 Ounces Lean Beef, 8 Ounces Red Skin Potatoes

Bedtime:

- 25 Grams Casein Protein Shake

Below is a sample meal Plan: (Non-Workout Days)

Breakfast:

- 4 Egg Whites with 4 Whole Eggs
- ¾ Cup Whole Grain Rolled Oats

Snack 1:

Two tablespoons of nut butter on celery

Lunch:

- 10 Ounces Grilled Chicken Breast
- 1 Cup Steamed Veggies with 1 tablespoon olive oil

Snack 2:

- 6 Ounces Lean Grass-Fed Beef
- Handful of Mixed Nuts

Dinner:

- 8 Ounces Wild-caught Cod, ½ Sliced Avocado
- Large Spinach Salad with Olive Oil or Coconut Oil Based Dressing

Bedtime:

- 25 Grams Casein Protein Shake

So, this is pretty much the model to becoming a pro bodybuilder.

Without kidding ourselves, we have to keep in mind that consistency and sticking to a thorough nutrition and workout plan for an extended period of time is the surest path to building a pro bodybuilder physique in the shortest period of time.

It is important that you remain regular with your nutrition and your workout schedule, just so you can produce the right setting for gaining lean muscle mass for the 1st 6 weeks, and maintaining all of your gains for the next 6 weeks, while at the same time, shedding a small percentage of body fat each week.

The eventual result will be a rock-solid physique with pro-standard conditioning!

How Do Pro Bodybuilders Track Their Progress

The very first step to evaluating your progress is figuring out what you want to achieve. Below, I will give you some ideas which you could use to measure your progress and stay on course with your workouts.

I mentioned earlier that the first step to evaluating your progress is to figure out where you want to be, or better put, what you want to achieve with your body.

This is where setting a realistic goal is vital.

Your goal could be as simple as desiring to grow your muscle mass at the end of an 8-week training cycle, or as sophisticated as desiring to be in the best pre-competition physique of your life over a 16-week cycle.

You also need to have some flexibility in your training plan. As you work out, it's important to feel your way into the workout.

By this, I mean you shouldn't allow the way you feel affect the way you go about your workout.

The surest way to measure how prepared you are to really train is to kick off your warm-ups and observe how they feel. If you find them satisfactory, move up, as per plan, and observe how the heavier weights feel.

If the weight feels lighter or, alternatively, if you feel stronger than normal, then go for the extra mile.

If not, do your best to stick to the game plan as much as you can. If the weights feel heavy and you don't feel strong enough, don't force it, simply do the best you can for that day.

That should do the trick! It worked for the pros, and it can work for you too. During the next training session, or maybe even the one after that, You would find that you'd do just fine.

You have to set a few realistic goals, both for the short and long term, and this is vital, even if you don't have plans of competing.

Also, you must realize that your goals have to be flexible too. This is because you may need to adjust your long term goal by using the short term results as guidelines, then reset both the short and long term goals as required.

It is vital that you reach high enough to stimulate you and your training, and it is also important that you don't overreach, as this can lead you to being discouraged.

One thing that can keep you in good stead over your training period is keeping an accurate training log. In your log, you can write down every rep you set to do per workout session.

You can also write down some short notes, such as, how you felt before training, how tired you were, maybe you didn't feel like training, maybe you had a cold, or had an injury, or experienced some emotions that could potentially discourage you from training that day.

Your training log should be close to you at all times as you train, and one of the first things you should do after a training set (after you remove whatever is restricting the blood flow to one or more parts of your body), is to write down what you did.

Your training log is important for setting up your training schedule, and for determining what works for you.

It's also important for figuring out how you're doing, and if it is necessary to make any changes in your short and long term training plans.

Pros make a habit of going through their training log all the time, in a bid to find out how much they have improved, by comparing their present routine to past ones, and then figuring out if they need to make any changes or just leave things as they are.

If you are making good progress, you can analyze the previous few months of training to see what you were doing that was working so well for you.

If you find sometimes that your training has become stale, then look back again to check what it was that wasn't working, and then compare to what you'd been doing during the successful phases in the past.

Keep in mind that when you're training, you shouldn't allow anyone or anything to be a distraction to you. Drop every problem at the gym or training room door because they will distract you from achieving your main purpose for being there. Which is to lift the weights in the best way you can, both physically and mentally.

If your training area doesn't cater to that, then switch spaces until you find a space and situation that is 100% suitable for you.

Leave your smartphone, tablet, or any other possible distractions, out of your training area. As for having conversations or pleasantries, well that's between you and your training partners, I am sure they are well aware when it's time to train and when it's time to talk.

You really don't have to have chats with anyone. You can give them a look that says "not now", and they'll leave you to focus on your training. You could always chat after your sessions.

The message here is that your workout time is for workout alone, and nothing else!

Maximizing Your Training

To maximize the anabolic, performance, and body composition effects of training, and to make sure the time and energy you invest in your training are not wasted, you need to be sure that your body has all the natural advantages that it can. You can make sure of this by using the right pre-training supplements.

Anabolic means the metabolic process that is characterized by molecular growth, such as the gaining of muscle mass. Hence, it simply refers to "muscle-building" in most common bodybuilding contexts.

Some pre-training supplements are formulated to influence pathways in the brain, for the sake of improving concentration and focus. Also to reduce the counterproductive effects of stress and distractions.

In order to get the best results from your training, you have to be primed, both physically and mentally.

Such pre-training supplements do not only improve focus and concentration while reducing distractions, but they can also improve neuromuscular functioning, which in turn improves the performance and intensity of your workouts.

They could act as musculoskeletal, neuromuscular, and central nervous system (CNS) optimizers.

The Central Nervous System

The human central nervous system is made up of the brain and spinal cord. These are found in the midline of the body, and they are guarded by the skull and vertebrae respectively.

This collection of billions of neurons is arguably the most complex object in the world.

The central nervous system along with the peripheral nervous system consists of a primary division of controls, which command all physical activities of a person.

Neurons of the central nervous system affect consciousness and mental activity, while spinal extensions of central nervous system neuron pathways affect skeletal muscles and organs in the human body.

Using these pre-training supplements, you can spend a shorter amount of time in the gym, and make your workouts more productive.

Some of these pre-training supplements will prepare you mentally, and allow you to workout effectively.

However, you still need to prepare your body properly to make the most of your improved mind control.

These should also produce anticatabolic and anabolic effects, by enhancing levels of testosterone and growth hormone (HGH), reducing protein breakdown, enhancing protein synthesis, and providing cell volumizing effects which improve muscle growth.

To add to this, they would also maximize energy levels, ATP and phosphocreatine (PC) functioning, as well as gluconeogenic, TCA Cycle flux, and other processes, which allows for more strength and stamina.

What Is The TCA Cycle?

The Krebs Cycle (Citric Acid Cycle, Tri-Carboxylic Acid Cycle, or TCA Cycle) is a complex sequence of biochemical enzymatic reactions, which is responsible for how much fat is lost through the dissipation of Acetyl-CoA.

If the TCA cycle slows down, then fat loss is restricted (fatty acids cannot be fully degraded). The Krebs Cycle involves oxidative metabolism of acetyl units and produces high-energy phosphate compounds, which serve as the main source of cellular energy.

The Krebs Cycle is named after Hans Krebs, a German chemist, whose research into the cellular utilization of glucose contributed immensely to the modern understanding of this aspect of metabolism.

As well, they should provide potent thermogenic and fat loss properties, increasing fat breakdown, and utilization, as well as a reduction of fat buildup.

Lastly, they should exert a potent antioxidant, buffering, and cytoprotective effect to decrease muscle tissue injury and soreness, and improve recovery.

Examples of these types of pre-training supplements include:

- Metabolic Diet's InControl
- Resolve

Tracking Your Progress: Measuring Body Composition

One of the surest ways to gauge your progress as far as body composition is concerned, is to look at yourself in the mirror and be your own honest judge.

Also assess your looks with the way your clothes fit, and you get a pretty good idea of whether or not you're making progress. To add to that, what people say about your looks is another measuring stick for progress.

Another means of tracking progress is by your workouts. If they're improving, and you're carrying more weight and/or doing more reps on a regular basis, then you're doing just fine. But, you have to be honest about your self-assessment!

It's important that your assessment of how well you're doing remains constant.

If you're carrying more weight in the bench press, but you're cheating by bouncing the bar off your chest, then you are not making any progress at all.

The issue with all of the progress-tracking measures I've pointed out so far is that they are subjective, and as such can lead you wrongly.

For this reason, you will need more objective measures for tracking how well you're doing.

One of the most effective objective measures of your progress, as far as body composition is concerned, is to find out how much fat your body is carrying, as a percentage of your total body weight.

The most accurate scientific means to determine your body fat percentage is by using hydrostatic weighing. This test is done in a special tank and compares your weight completely under (with all air exhaled out of your lungs) and out of water.

Hydrostatic weighing is based on the concept that the density and gravity of lean tissue is greater than that of fat tissue.

Hydrostatic weighing is the best means of measurement, but it is pretty expensive. It is also inconvenient and time-consuming.

Other means of checking body fat levels, such as magnetic resonance imaging (MRI) and the Bod Pod (a device that uses air displacement instead of water) are more convenient but are equally expensive and unavailable to a lot of trainees.

The most cost-effective means of measuring body fat percentage is by using anthropometric measurements.

By this means, measurements are taken with a measuring tape around areas where fat is usually distributed. These include the waist and thigh.

Specific equations are used to measure the percentage of body fat. Although these measurement methods are cheaper and easier to do, still, they are not as accurate.

Generally, you can measure body fat percentage with skinfold calipers. If this is done correctly, calipers are an accurate, cost-effective, and convenient means to measure the thickness of subcutaneous fat.

This technique involves gauging fat levels in the body by assessing levels at certain key fat depots with the skin calipers.

You should have the skin fold test performed by a professional. Alternatively, you can buy a set of calipers and do the test yourself.

Skinfold thickness measurements with calipers can be taken at multiple locations and then entered into a formula to give you a more accurate body fat assessment.

For instance, if you use the Accu-MeasureTM Calipers you can get a fairly good idea of the level of your body fat by taking skin density measurements of the suprailiac area.

Where Is Your Suprailiac Area?

This is the area at the top of your pelvis, right beside your waist, and just above the location of the hipbone. It is also about an inch forward, and midway between the hip joint and the bottom of the rib cage, above the iliac crest, in the midaxillary line.

It is true that knowing your body fat level is a step forward, but it doesn't give much information about your level of lean body mass. To get the real picture and accurately gauge your present status and progress, you need to find out more.

Quick Recap: Ways to Measure Body Composition Progress

- Use your mirror
- Check the way your clothes fit
- What people say about your physique

The Metabolic Index (MIDx) is the surest means to gauge your progress as far as body composition is concerned. The MIDx takes into detail, all the variables that other means cannot. It doesn't just address the height/weight issue, but also the levels of muscle mass and body fat.

Using the MIDx, you have a snap-shot of your body composition and progress. The MIDx is a ratio derived by factoring not only weight and height, but body fat percentage.

The Formula For MIDx

Figuring Out The MIDx: The Formula.

Body weight (in pounds) divided by the height (in inches) squared, then that result multiplied by 7250, and then those total results divided by the percent of body fat:

$\{(lbs / in^2;) \times 7{,}250 \} / BF \%$

Or, if you are using the Metric system:

$\{(kg / m^2;) \times 10.3 \} / BF \%$

For example, using pounds and inches, if your MIDx is 185 / 66⊃2; x 7250, divided by 10%.

{(185 / 4356) x 7,250 } / 10

Result: Your MIDx = 30.8

In reality, the MIDx is an indicator that when you're losing weight you're close to maintaining or even increasing lean body mass as you lose body fat.

Actually, the more lean body mass you have and the less fat, hence a better index. If someone loses a lot of weight but loses too much lean body mass, there wouldn't be much improvement in your index.

What that means is that even though the person has lost weight, they will most likely be looking pretty flabby, since they've lost the weight by also shedding muscle mass.

The important thing about the MIDx is that it will give you a starting point and from there an indication of how you're progressing every inch of the way.

Once you've confirmed your baseline MIDx, it would be easy to objectively see if you're making progress and if you're losing body fat, but not at the sacrifice of much needed muscle mass.

If the MIDx is increasing, even if it's very slight, then you're making good progress.

The higher the Metabolic Index, up to a point, the better your improvement, and the closer you are to reaching your desired goals.

The lower the Metabolic Index is, the more room you have for improvement, and a clear picture of just how much more you have to put in to reach your goals.

In summary, the best way for improving muscle mass and reducing body fat is by the means of manipulation.

This is done by triggering metabolic changes and altering the body's anabolic and catabolic hormones and growth factors.

By following a strict, well-planned training, diet, and nutritional supplement guideline, you'll add on impressive amounts of muscle mass and reduce your body fat down to the low single digits!

The Taylor Lautner Workout: Build Muscle Fast

Taylor Lautner, the world-famous actor, isn't a guy you would consider to be strong, but his career is very dependent on looking brawny.

Between the first and second Twilight movies, his character morphed into a big and strong werewolf.

This meant he needed to gain 30 pounds of muscle in a year. And he did that successfully.

Think about this, Taylor Lautner used to be a 5'10", 140-pound, bony teenager, but as of today, he's a well-carved fitness guru.

The point here is, If he can overcome his physical shortcomings, then you can do the same.

"Inexperience works to your advantage," this was said by Jordan Yuam, who is Lautner's trainer and the owner of Jordan's Virtual Fit Club. *"The less muscle you have, the easier it is to gain muscle mass more quickly."*

Your tactic should be to eat right and follow a smart, strategic workout regimen. *"Maximize your genetic potential,"* says Yuam. *"There's no reason you can't gain pounds of muscle in a year."*

Below is how to follow Taylor Lautner's model, and build strength at a very fast rate, without doing more than you have to.

Push Your Limits

To increase body size, your body needs to be comfortable with heavyweights. *"That's why I had Taylor 'taste' a much heavier weight,"* says Yuam, who used to stack a bar (or use dumbbells) with about 40% more weight than Lautner could normally lift 10 times.

So if you can carry about 120 pounds 10 times, give 170 pounds a try. Then, using a spotter, do only the lowering half of lifts.

"It's critical that your spotter be strong enough to lift the weight back up by himself," says Yuam.

For bench presses, it means slowly pulling down the weight to your chest. This allows your body adjust to the new weight, even before you're prepared to lift it. The program is challenging on your muscles, so limit your "tasting" to 2 or 3 sets of 5 reps every other week.

Vary Your Volume

Carrying more weight isn't always the best. To maximize gains, Lautner often varies reps and the amount of weight he carries.

"If you want a balanced body, you have to do that", says Yuam.

The more your muscles are pushed to adapt to a new program, the bigger they grow.

Instead of just doing 3 sets of 8 to 10 reps, for instance, reduce the weight and shoot for 4 sets of 15 reps once in a while.

A recent study in the Journal of Strength and Conditioning Research discovered that men who regularly varied their rep counts, and worked different muscle groups, Improved their bench strength by 28% and their leg-press strength by 43%.

Create Tension

Free weights are great, but they have a downside: Some parts of a lift are less tasking than others, so your muscles aren't being pushed consistently.

That's why Lautner usually connects giant rubber bands to a bar or dumbbell he's going to carry, and then fixes the bands to the base of a power rack or a pair of heavy dumbbells.

"The bands create more tension, making the lift harder and forcing your muscles to peak out at the top of the movement," Yuam says.

As a result, your body gathers more muscle fibers and works them harder, which speeds up growth. Bands can be bought in most gyms.

Cut Down on Cardio

"I was exercising so hard that I began to lose weight," says Lautner.

Sound great right? Well, not if you usually have trouble gaining muscle mass. When it's combined with weight training, cardio consumes strength and limits muscle building, especially if you spin your wheels for longer than 20 minutes before or after lifting. This is according to researchers at Stephen F. Austin State University in Texas.

So be wise not to push it too much. "If you're trying to build lean mass, concentrate on weight-lifting with the right technique and the right plan," says Yuam.

Don't Overwork Your Abs

"A lot of guys hit their abs every time they hit the gym," says Yuam.

"That's why so few of them have six-packs."

Your abs are similar to any other muscle group, and the same laws of muscle-building apply to them.

Do not overwork your abs. Lautner works his abs just 3 days per week and does a combination of programs to work his entire core.

"The result is a balanced, more detailed musculature," Yuam says.

One of his preferred combinations is the hanging leg raise to reverse crunch, holding for 7 to 10 seconds. This works your entire core and prevents a muffin top.

Step to the Side

Many weightlifting programs involve forward or backward movements. They don't work your body to explode in other directions.

Lautner requires a versatile body because he does his own stunts in his movies. Keep I mind that he still needs one for his everyday life.

Your basketball crossover move will be lame without it. The solution, Yuam says, is to perform side-to-side workouts in addition to traditional lifts. These will boost your ability to move in any path. For instance, do a few sets of lateral hops and lunges into every leg workout.

Have a Recovery Plan

Working out and eating are just two-thirds of the muscle-building equation. *"The other third is recovery,"* says Lautner.

He takes every third day off and never works out more than 5 days a week. *"If you constantly pound your muscles, they'll never have time to repair."*

Feed Your New Body

Your hard work starts in the gym, but your kitchen has an equally important role to play in your body transformation.

"How much you'll eat depends on how much you want to weigh", says nutrition expert Alan Aragon, M.S.

Set Your Daily Calorie Goal

Goal weight x (workout hours per week + 9.5) = daily number of calories

Example: Let's assume you weigh 180 pounds, and you want to add an extra 10 pounds of muscle. It means your target weight is 190 pounds.

If you plan to train 3 hours per week, then do this: Add 3 + 9.5, and then multiply the sum (12.5) by your goal weight of 190 pounds.

Result = 2,375. And that is your daily calorie goal.

Set Daily Nutritional Goals

Using this key, you will be able to determine how many grams of protein, fat, and carbohydrate you should consume per day.

goal weight = grams of protein

half your goal weight = grams of fat

daily calories - [(protein grams x 4) + (fat grams x 9)] / 4 = grams of carbs

Example: For your goal weight of 190 pounds, you should consume 190 grams of protein and 95 grams of fat.

For carbs: Multiply 190 by 4 (to get 760), and 95 by 9 (to get 855).

Add them together = 1,615. Now subtract that from your 2,375 daily calories, to get 760.

Then divide that by 4, Result = 190.

And That gives you your carb goal in grams.

Balance Your Meals

Be sure of the number of meals you'll have per day, and then break down your total allotment into equal portions. *"It doesn't matter if you eat three meals a day or six,"* says Aragon. *"As long as you stay within your guidelines, you'll see results."*

The Lautner's Formula for a 6-pack

Yuam helped Lautner gain about 30 pounds of lean muscle (and a well-carved six-pack) for the movie "New Moon".

He achieved this by working Lautner's core with a wide variety of exercises that work all the muscles found between the hips and chest.

Below are the workouts that made Lautner get the number-one spot on Access Hollywood's "Top 5 Hollywood Abs" list.

You can infuse them into your own training, and you will get results just as impressive as his.

1: Swiss Ball Pikes

Get into a pushup position with your arms totally straightened (your hands have to be slightly wider than, and in line with, your shoulders).

Place your shins on a Swiss ball, in a way that your body forms a straight line from your head to your ankles.

Without bending your knees, roll the Swiss ball toward your body by lifting your hips as high as you can. Stop, then return the ball to the starting position by lowering your hips and rolling the ball backward.

Perform 3 to 4 sets of 8 to 12 reps.

2: Reverse Crunches

Lie on your back, face up, with your palms facing downward. Bend your hips and knees to 90 degrees.

Lift your hips off the floor and crunch them inward. Stop, and then gradually lower your legs until your heels nearly touch the floor.

Perform 3 sets of 15 reps.

3: Swiss Ball Leg Curl

Lay on the floor with your calves on a Swiss ball and your arms by your sides. Squeeze your glutes to lift your hips off the floor so your body is in a straight line from your shoulders to your ankles. Stop for a second, and then bend your legs to roll the ball toward your butt.

Straighten your legs to roll the ball back out away from you, and then lower your body to the floor. Do 3 to 4 sets of 10 to 12 reps.

4: Hanging Leg Raises

Hold a chin-up bar with an overhand, shoulder-width grip (or use elbow supports, if available), then hang from the bar with your knees slightly bent and with your feet placed together.

At the same time, bend your knees, raise your hips, and curl your lower back beneath you as you raise your thighs toward your chest.

Stop when the fronts of your thighs reach your chest, then slowly lower your legs back to the starting position. Do 3 to 4 sets of 8 to 12 reps.

5: Prone Cobra

Lie facedown on the floor with your legs straight and your arms placed next to your sides, palms down. Then contract your glutes and the muscles of your lower back, and lift your head, chest, arms, and legs off the floor.

At the same time, rotate your arms so that your thumbs point toward the ceiling. At this time, your hips should be the only parts of your body touching the floor.

Maintain this position for 60 seconds, then take a one minute rest. Repeat the program three times.

Mike Tyson's Diet and Nutrition

Via almost every source, you will find pretty much the same diet and training method (which is why I feel comfortable sharing), but within each one, they come with some type of warning sign that makes sure to add words like: "potentially just rumors", "beyond belief", "almost too insane", and other phrases that just essentially mean the same.

As I mentioned earlier, a lot of different sources say much of the same, but this one from "The Fitness" seemed like the easiest to share (and read):

His nutritional diet consisted of 3000-4000 calories of carbohydrates and proteins to help build the right amount of body muscle and mass. Here's a brief breakdown of his diet plan:

Breakfast- Oatmeal with milk and vitamins.

Lunch- Rice with chicken breasts and orange juice.

Snack- Protein shake with 6 bananas.

Dinner- Pasta and steak with tropical juice.

This looks like a monster's diet, and Mike Tyson was nothing short of one. His boxing record is a testament to that fact.

Now whether or not he really had these exact meals, I suppose only he, and the people around him know for sure.

But then again we could say that about every single celebrity diet and workout.

These days, Tyson seems to eat more intuitively, while still stuffing his diet with protein, but skipping the tightly scheduled regime.

We see a lot of celebs opt for a sustainable approach like this.

Anthony Joshua's Diet Plan

Most regular-sized people need to look up when they meet Anthony Joshua. Being that he's 6ft 6 tall, that's barely surprising. What is surprising though, is that unlike most of Joshua's present heavyweight competitors, he is also one of the leanest men you're likely to come across.

It's pretty obvious that Joshua's muscular physique isn't totally crafted in the gym or the boxing ring, a decent part of it was gained right in the kitchen. He often talks about how he nourishes his body with his mother's African cooking, and the other approaches he employs in recent times.

Breakfast

The moment he wakes up, Joshua claims he starts his day with a simple glass of water, which, given that his job requires him to deliver knockout blows, makes sense.

According to a study published in Sports Medicine, a reduction in body water *"appears to consistently attenuate strength (by approximately two percent), power (by approximately three percent) and high-intensity endurance (by approximately 10 percent), suggesting alterations in total body water affect some aspect of force generation"*.

After he's had his glass of water, Joshua then moves on to eating a piece of fruit, which being loaded with vitamins, minerals, fiber, antioxidants, and tons of other nutrients is another smart move.

"Then I have porridge or something like that," says Joshua. Just like fruits, oats are loaded with vitamins, minerals, and fiber. They also provide an extra boost to anyone needing energy throughout the day, like Joshua does.

"A bowl of their slow-releasing, wholegrain goodness an hour before exercise ensures blood sugar levels remain steady through a workout, while providing enough energy to keep you going," says BBC Good Food editor, Roxanne Fischer.

Lunch

You wouldn't expect someone of Joshua's size to fuel themselves solely on water, fruit, and oats, so it's at lunch that the heavyweight boxer really gets into his A-game when it comes to eating.

"I'll go onto wild rice, some salmon, and a lot of vegs," Joshua tells MH. "[And then] I'll probably eat that again."

Joshua's choice of salmon is a smart one, as it provides enough protein, but a lot less saturated fat content.

A 2007 study published in Science Direct linked eating salmon to a hefty decrease in blood pressure, LDL cholesterol (AKA bad cholesterol), and a 25 percent reduction in coronary heart disease risk.

Similar to fruit, vegetables are filled with vitamins, minerals, and other vital nutrients that help keep your body healthy and functioning properly, and Joshua eats a lot of them. As for eating a meal of salmon, rice, and veggies twice? He clearly believes that there's absolutely nothing wrong with it.

Dinner

The idea of eating the same meal twice for lunch may not sound too appealing, but Joshua makes up for it at dinner time when he goes home to get a bite of his mum's African (Nigerian) cooking.

In an interview with the Nigerian online platform Oak TV, Joshua went as far as to put his success down to eating Nigerian dishes like pounded yam, eba and egusi. Obviously, he doesn't believe in completely switching his entire diet to a regimented plan, proving that the foods that you're familiar with can also be incorporated into a balanced, functional diet.

Top 10 Bodybuilding Supplements That Work

If your aim is to build muscle mass, shed fat, or just get healthy, you've most likely heard of bodybuilding supplements.

With so many sources of information, it could seem like a daunting task figuring out which ones actually work. This list recommends to you, the 10 best bodybuilding supplements to help you achieve your fitness goals.

Whey Protein - This is an easy and safe way to get your daily protein requirements. Not only can it help build the lean muscle you've been training so hard for in the gym, but it also has a great taste too.

BCAAs - Branched-chain amino acids (BCAAs) are excellent for reducing fatigue and maximizing workout intensity and duration. BCAAs also promote fat loss and muscle build-up, which will help make you look awesome!

Creatine Monohydrate – I have to say, this product is pretty powerful! Creatine is a bodybuilding supplement that aids performance and helps you attain your physique goals.

It has been proven to increase anabolic hormone levels, increase muscle strength, and reduce muscle protein breakdown.

Fish Oil – This supplement helps reduce inflammation, boost insulin resistance, and reduce the risk of cardiovascular disease.

L-Glutamine – L-Glutamine is one of the most effective bodybuilding supplements you can take to assist in building your joints and cartilage tissue.

It improves protein metabolism and maintains a strong immune system during hard training.

Multivitamins – Regardless of being a bodybuilder, it's always a good idea to supplement your meals with multivitamins. Being proactive in avoiding vitamin/mineral deficiencies is vital to a healthy and fit body.

Probiotic – We don't always consider gut health when the thought of bodybuilders crosses our minds, but healthy digestion is an important part of getting fit. A daily dose of probiotic helps protect your gut's healthy bacteria, which you need to process food optimally.

Glucosamine/Chondroitin – These bodybuilding supplements guard your joints and cartilage from the stress caused by heavy lifting.

These tissues provide the basis for strong muscles, so it's vital to infuse them in your supplement regimen.

Vitamin D3 – Popularly called the "sunshine vitamin", Vitamin D3 is gotten via exposure to sunlight or pills. It helps build healthy bones and it reduces the risk of certain diseases.

Magnesium – Magnesium is important for proper contraction of the muscle and function. It is mostly used by athletes to prevent muscle cramps and spasms that come with rigorous training.

How to Avoid Supplement Overdose and Misleading Bodybuilding Mistakes

Pros and Cons of 8 Popular Supplements

Once upon a time, pills, powders, and shakes promising to build muscles and improve energy levels were marketed strictly to bodybuilders and professional athletes. Nowadays, it seems like every gym, health food store, and supermarket stocks a wide range of supplements for anyone looking to lose weight, bulk up or gain stamina. While many weight-loss products target female consumers, a vast array of supplements are made specifically for men.

According to data from the 2007-2010 National Health and Nutrition Examination Survey, almost half of adult men take supplements. The most popular reasons they give for using supplements include the desire to improve overall health, maintain health, prevent health problems, and to boost immunity.

Most supplements marketed to men are advertised as guaranteed methods for improving athletic performance, helping in weight loss, and growing lean muscle. Despite these claims, it's important to bear in mind that supplements aren't regulated by the Food and Drug Administration (FDA), and it can be difficult to distinguish which ingredients are actually beneficial.

Here's a look at the pros and cons of some of the most common supplements for men.

1. Creatine

What it is: It is a natural substance that is converted in the body to help make adenosine triphosphate (ATP), which gives energy for muscle contractions.

Benefits: Creatine became popular for helping users improve athletic performance and gain lean body mass. It has been found to improve performance in high-intensity, short-duration exercises, and some research suggests it can help elevate resting testosterone levels.

Side effects: Stomach pain, nausea, diarrhea, muscle cramping, and temporary weight gain due to muscles retaining water.

2. Protein Powder

What it is: Protein powders come in various forms, but the most common are whey, soy, and casein. They can help increase the amount of complete, high-quality protein in a variety of food and beverages (healthy adults need 45 to 65 grams per day).

Benefits: Proteins facilitate crucial cellular functions, and complete proteins, like those in protein powders, contain all 20 amino acids necessary to form protein molecules. In the short term, high-protein diets have been shown to increase fat burn, increase satiety, and possibly lead to weight loss.

Side effects: High doses of protein powder can cause increased bowel movements, bloating, cramps, reduced appetite, fatigue, and headache.

3. Glutamine

What it is: Glutamine is an amino acid that the body produces naturally. It's important for removing excess waste products, healthy immune system function, and may play a role in normal brain function and digestion.

Benefits: Research suggests glutamine may help speed recovery from injuries and stop the breakdown of muscles and stimulate muscle tissue growth.

Side effects: Glutamine may be dangerous for some people, worsening cases of cirrhosis, mania, seizures, and other conditions. More common side effects include cough/hoarseness, frequent urge to defecate, and straining while passing stool.

4. Glucosamine

What it is: Glucosamine is a naturally occurring substance found in the fluid around joints and plays an important role in building cartilage.

Benefits: Some research suggests that glucosamine sulfate may help treat osteoarthritis, but there is little evidence of any significant effect.

Side effects: Nausea, heartburn, diarrhea, and constipation.

5. Prohormone Supplements, aka "Testosterone Boosters"

What they are: Prohormones are hormone precursors that the body can supposedly convert into the appropriate hormones. Prohormones of testosterone androstenedione, androstenediol, and dehydroepiandrosterone (DHEA) are commonly used by bodybuilders to get the benefits of anabolic steroids without the legal risk, but some prohormones are also outlawed.

Benefits: Current research indicates that prohormones have little or no proven benefit.

Side effects: Side effects are specific to each type of prohormone, but possible effects include acne, hair loss, liver damage, and enlarged breast tissue.

6. Animal Pak

What it is: According to the company's website, "Animal Pak features performance optimizers such as pyridoxine alpha-ketoglutarate (PAK), carnitine, lipotropics, L-arginine, alpha lipoic acid, eleuthero, and the like. In every pack, you get a vast arsenal of over 60 key ingredients that are delivered in the right amounts at the right time, every time."

Benefits: There is insufficient evidence for whether PAK enhances athletic performance. A small study found that taking alpha-ketoglutarate daily for five weeks improves athletic performance, but carnitine is considered unlikely to be effective for improving athletic performance.

Side effects: The specific side effects of Animal Pak are unknown, but the side effects of ingredients like PAK and carnitine include diarrhea, vomiting, nausea, cramps, and potential allergic reaction.

7. Nitric Oxide

What it is: Nitric oxide, a gas produced by the body, enables cells to communicate and can affect the release of hormones and adrenaline. Many pre-workout supplements contain L-arginine that the body converts into nitric oxide.

Benefits: There is insufficient evidence to demonstrate the effects of L-arginine on exercise performance.

Side effects: L-arginine can cause abdominal pain, bloating, diarrhea, gout, blood abnormalities, allergies, airway inflammation, worsening of asthma, and low blood pressure.

8. Caffeine

What it is: A crystalline compound that stimulates the central nervous system, caffeine is a common ingredient in many pre-workout supplements and is thought to increase energy and enhance performance.

Benefits: Caffeine has been shown to reduce feelings of exertion and improve performance during activities like cycling, running, soccer, and golfing, but doesn't seem to improve performance in short-term, high-intensity exercise such as sprinting and lifting.

Side effects: Caffeine can cause insomnia, nervousness and restlessness, stomach irritation, nausea and vomiting, increased heart rate and respiration, and other side effects. Caffeine can make sleep disorders worse, and larger doses might cause headaches, anxiety, agitation, chest pain, and ringing in the ears.

A word of Caution When Using Supplements

The supplement market is flooded with products commonly marketed by untrained salespeople, with little to no discussion about potential side effects. In addition to the monetary cost of supplements, which can be prohibitively high for some, the side effects can be serious, and in some cases, permanent.

Always consult a medical provider before initiating a new supplement regimen. Your health care provider will be able to discuss the pros and cons of supplementation with you in a more equitable way, and possibly offer safer alternatives.

5 Natural Supplements You Need for Real Muscle Gains

Any trainer, nutritionist, or bodybuilder worth their salt knows one thing for sure: Building muscle takes more than just pumping iron.

Of course, you're not going to experience any serious gains in muscle strength or size if you don't exercise at least a little, but relying just on lifting heavy weights doesn't always guarantee you'll wake up looking like the Hulk.

Serious bodybuilders know the importance of fueling muscle growth properly. Eating a high protein, a clean diet full of healthy fats and veggies may help you lose fat while simultaneously giving your muscles the nutrients they need to repair and rebuild. But sometimes there's only so much muscular hypertrophy or muscle building one can achieve when relying on a whole-foods diet.

You need a little help. That's why many gym-goers turn to supplements to help them achieve their goals, whether it be fat loss, an increase in muscle mass, or greater endurance.

But not all protein powders and pre-workout mixes are created equal. Check out my five favorite natural supplements for real muscle gains.

Glutamine

A common amino acid found in muscle tissue, glutamine sources are depleted when muscles are worked to exhaustion. That can lead to decreased strength, endurance, and recovery. Not good if you're trying to get big! Supplementing with glutamine may increase muscle tone.

Collagen protein

Already the darling of the Paleo world, dietary collagen is a building block of healthy muscle, tendons, ligaments, and fascia, making it an important supplement for recovery. Strenuous exercise like repeatedly lifting heavy weights (or any type of endurance training, for that matter) can help you build muscle. But this comes at the price of breaking down the collagen in your body, meaning those tissues can't rebuild themselves as quickly. Adding it to your diet may help tendons and ligaments. Add a scoop or two into your morning smoothie, or take it in pill form.

MCT oil

The medium-chain triglycerides that makeup MCT oil deliver energy straight to the muscles you'll work in the gym. Plus, because growing muscles increase metabolic rate—which means you're burning more calories—most lifters need to increase their daily calories, too. MCTs are an easy way to get more calories per day without feeling like you're force-feeding.

Organic whey protein

With 20 grams of protein per serving, whey protein is a supplement of choice for most professional and new athletes alike. Not only does protein help support muscle mass, but whey protein offers branch chain amino acids, another building block of muscle. We opt for this organic version because it tastes great and doesn't have any unnecessary fillers. Plus, it's made from whey concentrate which means it's less processed than whey isolate products.

Plant-based protein powder

Wanna get your daily dose of protein but find that whey gives you "bathroom problems"? First off, that's pretty normal. Because lactose and casein are two of the main components of protein in whey, they can cause some serious indigestion and bloating in those with a milk sensitivity.

Check out this raw vegan plant protein. At 30 grams of protein per serving, it outperforms its whey protein counterparts. Plus, it naturally contains probiotic powers that help keep gut bacteria healthy—which is super important if you're downing more food than usual or trying to Performance.

Getting into awesome shape doesn't require crazy chemical-laden powders and pills, you'll find that you can get the same results without the detrimental side effects by going clean and organic. Here's to your fittest year yet!

How to Build Muscle without Supplements

Disease, aging, and a sedentary lifestyle break down your soft tissues. Many methods let you build muscle and prevent this loss. Yet muscle-building drugs can cause side effects. Fortunately, there are natural ways to increase muscle mass without supplements. Learning these effective and safe methods can help you slow aging and fight disease and muscle breakdown.

Understand Muscle Anatomy

You have more than 600 muscles. Many of them develop in pairs: right and left. Trainers mostly concern themselves with the large skeletal muscles you use during a workout. Examples include the biceps muscles in your upper arms and the quadriceps muscles in your lower legs.

Understand Muscle Physiology

Your muscles do a lot more than you think. In addition to generating force, they also remove dietary sugar from your bloodstream and keep your body active — metabolically — as you rest. Given these important roles, everyone should want to build more muscle. Scientists call the muscle-building, or anabolic, process hypertrophy.

You need to alter the balance between muscle protein synthesis and muscle protein breakdown to attain hypertrophy, according to a 2018 report in Nutrients. Exercising and increasing your protein intake will help you reach this goal. Athletes often supplement protein in creative ways, but a well-balanced, omnivorous diet achieves the same effect. Thus, it's possible to build muscles without supplements.

Know Muscle Wasting in Aging

Doctors call the age-related decline in muscle mass sarcopenia. This process is inevitable. If you live long enough, you will have to face it. Yet you can slow the decay by building muscle.

Unfortunately, some people cannot easily build muscle — they have anabolic resistance. This medical condition appears most often in older people, and it's more than just their age. This group has added risk factors for anabolic resistance, such as chronic inflammation, insulin resistance and lipotoxicity, according to a 2013 report in JAMDA.

Know Muscle Wasting in Disease

Muscle wasting occurs in many diseases as well. This process, cachexia, appears in 50 percent of all cancer cases. Unfortunately, cancer patients face two anabolic problems: Cancer directly causes muscle loss, and chemotherapy exacerbates this loss.

Cancer patients also have difficulty overcoming muscle loss. Like older people, cancer patients often experience anabolic resistance and other medical complications. Hospitalized patients also find it challenging to exercise, given the physical and mental drain of a life-changing illness. Finally, hospitals rarely have exercise equipment readily available for patients to use.

Disease, aging and a sedentary lifestyle break down your soft tissues. Many methods let you build muscle and prevent this loss. Yet muscle-building drugs can cause side effects. Fortunately, there are natural ways to increase muscle mass without supplements. Learning these effective and safe methods can help you slow aging and fight disease and muscle breakdown.

Understand Muscle Anatomy

You have more than 600 muscles. Many of them develop in pairs: right and left. Trainers mostly concern themselves with the large skeletal muscles you use during a workout. Examples include the biceps muscles in your upper arms and the quadriceps muscles in your lower legs.

In a paper by Palacky University, the authors described a way to increase muscle mass without supplements. They also show how making this change improves your health and helps you fight disease.

Understand Muscle Physiology

Your muscles do a lot more than you think. In addition to generating force, they also remove dietary sugar from your bloodstream and keep your body active — metabolically — as you rest. Given these important roles, everyone should want to build more muscle. Scientists call the muscle-building, or anabolic, process hypertrophy.

You need to alter the balance between muscle protein synthesis and muscle protein breakdown to attain hypertrophy, according to a 2018 report in Nutrients. Exercising and increasing your protein intake will help you reach this goal. Athletes often supplement protein in creative ways, but a well-balanced, omnivorous diet achieves the same effect. Thus, it's possible to build muscles without supplements.

Know Muscle Wasting in Aging

Doctors call the age-related decline in muscle mass sarcopenia. This process is inevitable. If you live long enough, you will have to face it. Yet you can slow the decay by building muscle.

Unfortunately, some people cannot easily build muscle — they have anabolic resistance. This medical condition appears most often in older people, and it's more than just their age. This group has added risk factors for anabolic resistance, such as chronic inflammation, insulin resistance and lipotoxicity, according to reports.

Muscle wasting occurs in many diseases as well. This process, cachexia, appears in 50 percent of all cancer cases. Unfortunately, cancer patients face two anabolic problems: Cancer directly causes muscle loss, and chemotherapy exacerbates this loss.

Cancer patients also have difficulty overcoming muscle loss. Like older people, cancer patients often experience anabolic resistance and other medical complications. Hospitalized patients also find it challenging to exercise, given the physical and mental drain of a life-changing illness. Finally, hospitals rarely have exercise equipment readily available for patients to use.

Know Muscle Wasting When You're Sedentary

Sedentary people of any age also experience muscle wasting. Automation has simplified many jobs, and even a short hospital stay can quickly decrease muscle mass. Children are far less active today than in years past, and this trend seems likely to continue.

Many obstacles prevent sedentary children and adults from becoming active, according to a 2017 article in Obesity Reviews. The authors of this report describe 77 barriers to exercise, ranging from childcare availability to safety issues. Fortunately, they also describe a few facilitators of exercise to help create an environment where exercise naturally and easily happens.

Recognize the Consequences

The muscle loss found in sedentarism, disease, and aging has dire consequences. Losing muscle puts you at risk for disease and even death, according to a 2018 paper in Medicine and Science in Sports and Exercise. This relationship holds true regardless of issues like smoking and disease, and it's apparent even in younger people.

Identify the Treatments

The obesity epidemic has at least one positive effect. It has brought attention to the problems associated with inactivity. This attention has led many companies to offer solutions. You can use these treatments for building muscle in addition to losing weight.

Most muscle-building treatments feature anabolic substances. However, there's an increasing interest in natural treatments like exercise, vibration and light. These effective and safe methods provide a healthy way to build muscle without supplements.

Do Sports for Muscle Mass

Playing team sports provides many health benefits. Sports increase heart health and decrease body fat. They also evoke feelings of camaraderie and joy. A 2019 report in the European Journal of Sport Science looked at changes in muscle mass in younger men as they returned to competition.

These researchers tracked the players' body composition and metabolic rate as they began playing rugby. Compared to baseline, competing for 14 weeks increased the players' muscle mass and decreased their body fat. Playing rugby didn't alter their metabolic rate.

Chapter 5 Summary

There are many successful bodybuilders around the world, all of them achieved their aim with almost the same techniques and principles, even though they are slightly different.

Many follow a specific diet with proper use of supplements, however, some achieved their goal naturally, without the use of any supplements.

Chapter 6: Bodybuilding Myths

Those who are new to the world of bodybuilding must have heard many myths regarding weight gain, weight loss, and muscle building. As a newbie, you u may be inclined to believe everything you hear in the gym, even the ones that are not true!

Actually, many of those who you hear these myths from have limited knowledge of how the human body responds to training.

This is not to say they have no idea what they are talking about, it simply means you shouldn't believe everything you hear. It also means you should do some investigation yourself to discover the truth about how exercises will transform your body.

Failed to find out the truth will lead you to make so many mistakes during your quest for a well-carved physique. This will of course amount to wasted time, effort, and gym membership fees!

So, what are the most common myths you have heard? I have taken out the time to pick out the most popular of them all and share with you, so keep reading.

Here they are below.

High repetitions burn fat while low repetitions build muscle

To make your muscles bigger, then progressive overload is needed. This means that you are required to do more reps than you did during your last training session for that particular exercise.

The truth is, if you do the same amount of reps to ring every training session, then nothing will change. Basically, if the weight on the bar isn't increased, you wouldn't find any changes in your physique.

If you perform the same amount of reps at each workout nothing will change on you, also "if the weight doesn't change on the bar nothing will change on you".

You need to become stronger

Definition has two characteristics, muscle size and a low incidence of body fat.

To shed body you must drop your calorie intake. The high repetition exercise will burn some calories, but wouldn't it be better to fast walk to burn these off?

Better still, make use of the low reps to gain muscle, which will elevate your metabolism and burn more calories (less fat).

Vegetarians can't build muscle

This is another false myth because they can!

Strength workouts with supplementation of soy Protein Isolate has proven to increase solid bodyweight. Studies have revealed that athletic performance is not hindered by following a meat-free diet, and people strength training and consuming only soy protein isolate as a protein source were able to build lean muscle mass.

Strength Training will make you look masculine

If it is not your intention to bulk up from strength training, then you won't.

Gaining muscle is a long, hard, and slow process. Your strength-training regime paired with quality food will determine how much you will bulk up.

Of course, you can consume whatever you wish if you don't care how you want to look. Working out does not give you an open license to consume as many calories as you want.

Although you will burn more calories if you workout than someone who doesn't, you still need to balance your energy intake with your energy expenditure.

If you take a week off you will lose most of your gains

Taking one or two weeks off occasionally will not harm your training. By taking this time off every eight to ten weeks in between strength training cycles it has the habit of refreshing you and to heal those small niggling injuries. By having longer layoffs you do not actually lose muscle fibers, just volume through not training; any size loss will be quickly re-gained.

By eating more protein I can build bigger muscles

Building muscle mass involves two things, progressive overload to stimulate muscles beyond their normal levels of resistance and eating more calories than you can burn off. With all the hype about high protein diets lately and because muscle is made largely of protein, it's easy to believe that protein is the best fuel for building muscle. However, muscles work on calories that should predominately be derived from carbohydrates.

If I'm not sore after a workout, I didn't work out hard enough

Post-workout soreness is not an indication of how good the exercise or strength-training session was for you. The fitter you are at a certain activity, the less soreness you will experience after. As soon as you change an exercise, use a heavier weight or do a few more reps you place extra stress on that body part and this will cause soreness.

Resistance training doesn't burn fat

Nothing could be further from the truth. Muscle is a metabolically active tissue and has a role in increasing the metabolism. The faster metabolism we have the quicker we can burn fat. Cardio exercise enables us to burn calories whilst exercising but does little else for fat loss afterwards.

Weight training enables us to burn calories whilst exercising but also helps us to burn calories whilst at rest. Weight training encourages muscle growth and the more lean muscle mass we possess, the more fat we burn though an increased and elevated metabolism.

No pain no gain

This is one myth that hangs on and on. Pain is your body signaling that something is wrong. If you feel real pain during a workout, stop your workout and rest. To develop muscle and increase endurance you may need to have a slight level of discomfort, but that's not actual pain.

Taking steroids will make me huge

Not true, strength training and correct nutrition will grow muscle. Taking steroids without training will not make you muscular. Most steroids allow faster muscle growth through greater recovery, while others help increase strength which allows for greater stress to be put onto a muscle. Without food to build the muscle or training to stimulate it nothing will happen. Most of the weight gain seen with the use of some steroids is due to water retention and is not actual muscle.

Strength training won't work your heart

Wrong! Strength training with short rest periods will increase your heartbeat well over a hundred beats per minute. For example, performing a set of breathing squats and you can be guaranteed that your heart will be working overtime and that your entire cardiovascular system will be given a great overall body workout.

Any intensive weightlifting routine that lasts for 20 minutes or more is a great workout for your heart and the muscles involved.

I can gain muscle and lose fat at the same time

Wrong. Only a few gifted people with superb genetics and on steroids can increase muscle size while not putting on body fat. But for the average hard gainer, they have to increase their muscle mass to its maximum potential and then cut down their body fat percentage to achieve the desired shape.

In conclusion, simple basic principles that apply to all weight and muscle gain such as progressive overload, variable frequency of reps and high-intensity workouts are the way to go.

Weightlifting Myths You Need To Stop Believing

Weightlifting is a big part of bodybuilding, it also comes s with some myths. Let us take a look at them below.

It's best to work one muscle group a day

I'd say this is one of the biggest weightlifting myths there is. Whether you're working one muscle group or several, one method is not evidentially better than the other.

The amount of muscle groups you train in one day depends on your goals. If you're a bodybuilder and want to just target biceps then fair enough, but if you want to just get fitter, you might target more of your upper body. Some people will do whole upper body days and whole lower body days.

If I created a training split of chest, back, arms, and legs for someone who was bodybuilding, but someone else wanted a push, pull and legs program – either one is fine if it gets people in the gym. Look at Arnold Schwarzenegger – he continually split trained chest, back, and biceps all on the same day and he turned out ok.

Another important point to make is that when you're doing push and pull exercises, you're working more than one muscle group anyway – back exercises work your biceps, whereas chest and shoulders exercises work your triceps. These muscle groups are part and parcel of any weightlifting program, so there's no need to isolate them.

Lifting heavy is the only way to look big

100% not true. Years ago, there were circus strongmen who'd pick up a heavy iron dumbbell and lift it over their head, but they never looked in great shape. Then Charles Atlas came along – he basically pioneered the idea of lifting a fairly heavyweight 10 times, instead of lifting as heavy as you could once.

That's the method weightlifters of today use for hypertrophy, which is the term for an increase in muscle size. If size is what you want, you do 8-12 reps, whereas if you're strength training, you'll do around 3-5. Again, it all depends on your goals, but lifting heavy is not the only way to build muscle.

Most people gain size through time under tension and slow eccentric lowering followed by four seconds down and one second up – all of which is only really possible by performing more reps with lighter weights. Lifting lighter but doing more reps is also safer on your joints. That said, if you're bodybuilding, it still needs to be challenging – the last couple of reps for each set should be a struggle.

Powerlifters, on the other hand, will lift up and down a lot quicker and as long as the weight's off the ground, the lift's counted. But there's no right or wrong way – both methods work. If you look at the British bodybuilder Dorian Yates, he did high intensity, heavyweight training of 1-4 reps, whereas Arnold Schwarzenegger did high volume sets of up to 15 reps.

Weightlifting doesn't improve your cardiovascular health

I don't agree with this at all. What I'd say to anyone who agrees is, put your hand on your heart after a leg day and get back to me. Any form of exercise causes your blood vessels to vasodilate, or widen, which provides more blood to the muscle and works the heart.

You can do cardio with weights as part of circuit training, so weightlifting and cardiovascular health are not mutually exclusive. After any tough session, you should be able to find your pulse and know that you've worked hard. An ideal BPM (beats per minute) for a relatively fit man performing a moderate intensity workout should be around 140 reps

Doing crunches gets rid of belly fat

I get so many clients saying: 'I need to do more crunches because this belly's still not going down'. The only way that belly is going down is by being in a calorie deficit. So, if you go to the gym and lift weights, that's going to help trim belly fat. If you do cardio, that's going to help trim body fat.

But you don't get to decide which part of your body loses the most fat – that's down to genetics. We've all got abs, you just need a low amount of body fat to reveal them. While crunches will make them more prominent and enhance core strength, you can't target fat loss purely through sit-ups.

If your goal is to bulk up and you need calories to supplement that, concentrate on getting bigger, and once you've reached your target or got close to where you want to be, then you can shed body fat. But building muscle and losing body fat is very difficult, unless you're a teenage boy with hormones through the roof, using steroids, or one of these very lucky people with good genetics.

When I get people through the door, a lot of them want to get bigger yet still lose body fat. That might happen in the first few sessions if they've never lifted before, but in the long term, you can't sustain it.

Resting between sets is critical

There are two schools of thought on this. Supersets, where you do a set of one exercise followed immediately by another, allow you to maximize the intensity of your workout and increase muscle tension, which is conducive to bodybuilding.

However, you need a fair amount of rest in between sets for consistency and to stop yourself burning out. You don't need to keep doing one exercise then resting, but recovery is essential for helping you give each set maximum effort. The amount of rest you take is obviously goal-specific. Powerlifters tend to rest for up to three minutes, bodybuilders will rest for around 50 seconds, and people doing fat loss circuits will have 15-20 seconds rest.

Ironically, though, the most important rest period is after a workout – that's when you grow, you don't grow in the gym.

Muscle will turn to fat if you stop lifting

That's scientifically impossible. Fat can't turn into muscle and vice versa. Fat is broken down into lipids, whereas muscle is attached to the bone. They're two completely different things.

Where this idea of turning muscle to fat comes from is, if you're a bodybuilder like Ronnie Coleman or Jay Cutler and you're used to having 6,000 calories a day, but then you stop going to the gym, you've still got an appetite for 6,000 calories a day. The problem is, you don't have the expenditure of weights and cardio you were doing.

So, when people think muscle has turned to fat, it hasn't – they've just gained additional fat because they're not burning off enough calories. After a few weeks of not training, the muscle will start to break down and waste away, but it doesn't 'turn into' fat.

By the same token, if someone was overweight, trained at the gym and then looked ripped, it wouldn't be because their fat's turned to muscle, it'd be because they'd lost the fat that was covering the muscle.

Myths about Building Arms

Here you will find some of the biggest myths regarding building arms.

You Won't Build Huge Arms With High Reps

This is not only an outright lie but quite on the contrary, utilizing a high-rep scheme is an excellent way to build big arms.

When we say high reps we think about doing 15-20 reps per set. When you do isolation movements like biceps curls or triceps pushdowns, it is best if you don't go below 12 reps per set.

But that's just a suggestion. You can train in every rep range you choose. Anything between 6-20 reps works.

You Only Need To Do Isolation Exercises

This is completely false and needs to be debunked. If you walked into any gym in the country and looked around you would see a lot of guys doing tons of curls and pushdowns and yet they still have tiny arms.

As with the big muscle groups, it's recommended that you train your arms with heavy, compound movements as well. That's the fastest way to pack on muscle mass. You build big arms with pull-ups/chin-ups, dips, and push-ups.

Isolation Exercises Don't Work

This may sound a bit contradictory to the previous myth on our list, but just because isolation exercises shouldn't be the focus of your training program, doesn't mean they are entirely useless.

If building big arms is what you're after, then you can dedicate 10% of your workout on isolation movements. For example, for every nine sets of chin-ups, you can do a single set of barbell curls. That's a 90/10 ratio.

And there's something important to point out here. The more muscle mass you have, the more isolation training you're allowed to do. That's because there's a genetic limit to how big you can get.

If you're skinny and you still have a long way to go when it comes to building muscle, then your primary focus should be compound movements to build muscle mass as fast as possible.

If you've been training seriously for less than 2 years, you can do the 90/10 split. If you've been lifting for 3-5 years, then you can go for an 80/20 split.

If you are a hulk and have been lifting for more than 6 years, you can change this ratio to 60/40, meaning for every 6 sets of chin-ups you can do 4 sets of barbell curls.

The conclusion is that the more experienced you are, the more benefit you can get from isolation work.

You Need To Train Using High Volume

Even though training with a high volume can help you build big arms, it's not necessary.

Why is that? Because the muscles comprising the arm, the biceps, and triceps are small muscles and do not need a big amount of stimulation in order to grow.

If you train with too much volume, you could prevent them from recovering properly.

You Cannot Build Big Arms With A Full-Body Training Program

Full-body training has become very popular in recent years and it's a great way to build muscle all over your body. But it's not a great way to build huge arms.

You need a specialized training program that would specifically target your arms. The most important thing you need to remember when it comes to building big arms is that training frequency is key.

Your primary focus should be on stimulating the muscles as often as possible within a time frame in which you allow your muscle to properly recover.

That's why if you want to build big arms you need to target them intensely and frequently. Here's a sample workout you could try that employs both full-body training principles with an emphasis on arms.

Myths about Weight Loss

There are many my about weight-loss too. Below are some of the most popular ones.

All calories are equal

The calorie is a measurement of energy. All calories have the same energy content.

However, this does not mean that all calorie sources have the same effects on your weight.

Different foods go through different metabolic pathways and can have vastly different effects on hunger and the hormones that regulate your body weight.

For example, a protein calorie is not the same as a fat or carb calorie.

Replacing carbs and fat with protein can boost your metabolism and reduce appetite and cravings, all while optimizing the function of some weight-regulating hormones.

Also, calories from whole foods like fruit tend to be much more filling than calories from refined foods, such as candy.

Also, calories from whole foods like fruit tend to be much more filling than calories from refined foods, such as candy.

Supplements can help you lose weight

The weight loss supplement industry is massive.

Various companies claim that their supplements have dramatic effects, but they're rarely very effective when studied.

The main reason that supplements work for some people is the placebo effect. People fall for the marketing tactics and want the supplements to help them lose weight, so they become more conscious of what they eat.

That said, a few supplements have a modest effect on weight loss. The best ones may help you shed a small amount of weight over several months.

Obesity is about willpower, not biology

It is inaccurate to say that your weight is all about willpower.

Obesity is a very complex disorder with dozens — if not hundreds — of contributing factors.

Numerous genetic variables are associated with obesity, and various medical conditions, such as hypothyroidism, PCOS, and depression, can increase your risk of weight gain.

Your body also has numerous hormones and biological pathways that are supposed to regulate body weight. These tend to be dysfunctional in people with obesity, making it much harder to lose weight and keep it off.

The leptin signal is supposed to tell your brain that it has enough fat stored. Yet, if you're resistant to leptin, your brain thinks that you're starving.

Trying to exert willpower and consciously eating less in the face of the leptin-driven starvation signal is incredibly difficult.

Of course, this doesn't mean that people should give up and accept their genetic fate. Losing weight is still possible — it's just much harder for some people.

Eat less, move more

Body fat is simply stored energy.

To lose fat, you need to burn more calories than you take in.

For this reason, it seems only logical that eating less and moving more would cause weight loss.

While this advice works in theory, especially if you make a permanent lifestyle change, it's a bad recommendation for those with a serious weight problem.

Most people who follow this advice end up regaining any lost weight due to physiological and biochemical factors.

A major and sustained change in perspective and behavior is needed to lose weight with diet and exercise. Restricting your food intake and getting more physical activity isn't enough.

Instructing someone with obesity to simply eat less and move more is like telling someone with depression to cheer up or someone with alcoholism to drink less.

Carbs make you fat

Low-carb diets can aid weight loss, in many cases, this happens even without conscious calorie restriction. As long as you keep carb intake low and protein intake high, you'll lose weight.

Even so, this does not mean that carbs cause weight gain. While the obesity epidemic started around 1980, humans have been eating carbs for a very long time.

In fact, whole foods that are high in carbs are very healthy.

On the other hand, refined carbs like refined grains and sugar are definitely linked to weight gain.

Fat makes you fat

Fat provides around 9 calories per gram, compared with only 4 calories per gram of carbs or protein.

Fat is very calorie-dense and commonplace in junk foods. Yet, as long as your calorie intake is within a healthy range, fat does not make you fat.

Additionally, diets that are high in fat but low in carbs have been shown to cause weight loss in numerous studies.

Eating breakfast is necessary to lose weight

Studies show that breakfast skippers tend to weigh more than breakfast eaters.

However, this is probably because people who eat breakfast are more likely to have other healthy lifestyle habits.

In fact, a 4-month study in 309 adults compared breakfast habits and found no effect on weight whether the participants ate or skipped breakfast.

It's also a myth that breakfast boosts metabolism and that eating multiple small meals makes you burn more calories throughout the day.

It's best to eat when you're hungry and stop when you're full. Eat breakfast if you want to, but don't expect it to have a major effect on your weight.

Fast food is always fattening

Not all fast food is unhealthy.

Because of people's increased health consciousness, many fast-food chains have started offering healthier options.

Some, such as Chipotle, even focus exclusively on serving healthy foods.

It's possible to get something relatively healthy at most restaurants. Most cheap fast-food restaurants often provide healthier alternatives to their main offerings.

These foods may not satisfy the demands of every health-conscious individual, but they're still a decent choice if you don't have the time or energy to cook a healthy meal.

Weight loss diets work

The weight loss industry wants you to believe that diets work.

However, studies show that dieting rarely works in the long-term. Notably, 85% of dieters end up gaining the weight back within a year.

Additionally, studies indicate that people who diet are most likely to gain weight in the future.

Thus, dieting is a consistent predictor of future weight gain — not loss (17Trusted Source).

The truth is that you probably shouldn't approach weight loss with a dieting mindset. Instead, make it a goal to change your lifestyle permanently and become a healthier, happier, and fitter person.

If you manage to increase your activity levels, eat healthier, and sleep better, you should lose weight as a natural side effect. Dieting probably won't work in the long term.

People with obesity are unhealthy and thin people are healthy

It's true that obesity increases your risk of several chronic illnesses, including type 2 diabetes, heart disease, and some cancers.

However, plenty of people with obesity are metabolically healthy — and plenty of thin people have these same chronic diseases.

It seems to matter where your fat builds up. If you have a lot of fat in your abdominal area, you're at a greater risk of metabolic disease.

Diet foods can help you lose weight

A lot of junk food is marketed as healthy.

Examples include low-fat, fat-free, and processed gluten-free foods, as well as high-sugar beverages.

You should be skeptical of any health claims on food packaging, especially on processed items. These labels usually exist to deceive — not inform.

Some junk food marketers will encourage you to buy their fattening junk food. In fact, if the packaging of a food tells you that it's healthy, there's a chance it's the exact opposite.

The bottom line

If you're trying to lose weight, you may have heard a lot of the same myths. You may have even believed some of them, as they're hard to avoid in Western culture.

Notably, most of these myths are false.

Instead, the relationship between food, your body, and your weight is very complex.

Chapter 6 Summary

Every newcomer to bodybuilding would have heard a thousand myths about weight gain, dieting, building abs, and/or building biceps.

Sadly, many of these myths are not true, and they can be misleading, causing trainees to make mistakes in their workout and dieting plans.

Always seek professional advice or conduct some thorough research and get the facts right before you believe these myths.

Chapter 7: How to Boost Hormones

Human growth hormone (HGH) is an important hormone produced by your pituitary gland.

Also known as growth hormone (GH), it plays a key role in growth, body composition, cell repair, and metabolism.

HGH also boosts muscle growth, strength, and exercise performance, while helping you recover from injury and disease.

Low HGH levels may decrease your quality of life, increase your risk of disease, and make you gain fat (9Trusted Source).

Optimal levels are especially important during weight loss, injury recovery, and athletic training (10Trusted Source, 11Trusted Source, 12Trusted Source, 13Trusted Source).

Interestingly, your diet and lifestyle choices can significantly affect your HGH levels (6Trusted Source, 14Trusted Source).

Here are 11 evidence-based ways to increase human growth hormone (HGH) levels naturally.

Lose body fat

The amount of belly fat you carry is directly related to your HGH production

Those with higher levels of belly fat will likely have impaired HGH production and an increased risk of disease.

One study observed that those with three times the amount of belly fat as the control group had less than half their amount of HGH.

Another study monitored the 24-hour release of HGH and found a large decline in those with more abdominal fat.

Interestingly, research suggests that excess body fat affects HGH levels more in men. However, lowering body fat is still key for both genders.

Fast intermittently

Studies show that fasting leads to a major increase in HGH levels.

One study found that 3 days into a fast, HGH levels increased by over 300%. After 1 week of fasting, they had increased by a massive 1,250%.

Other studies have found similar effects, with double or triple HGH levels after just 2–3 days of fasting.

However, continuous fasting is not sustainable in the long term. Intermittent fasting is a more popular dietary approach that limits eating to brief time periods.

Multiple methods of intermittent fasting are available. One common approach is a daily 8-hour eating window with a 16-hour fast. Another involves eating only 500–600 calories 2 days per week.

Intermittent fasting can help optimize HGH levels in two main ways. First, it can help you drop body fat, which directly affects HGH production.

Second, it'll keep your insulin levels low for most of the day, as insulin is released when you eat. Research suggests that insulin spikes can disrupt your natural growth hormone production.

One study observed large differences in HGH levels on the fasting day compared with the eating day.

Shorter 12–16-hour fasts likely help as well, though more research is needed to compare their effects with full-day fasts.

Try an arginine supplement

When taken alone, arginine may boost HGH.

Though most people tend to use amino acids like arginine alongside exercise, several studies show little or no increase in HGH levels.

However, studies have observed that taking arginine on its own — without any exercise —significantly increases levels of this hormone.

Other non-exercise studies also support the use of arginine to boost HGH.

One study examined the effects of taking either 45 or 114 mg of arginine per pound (100 or 250 mg per kg) of body weight, or around 6–10 or 15–20 grams per day, respectively.

It found no effect for the lower dose, but participants taking the higher dose experienced around a 60% increase in HGH levels during sleep.

Reduce your sugar intake

An increase in insulin is associated with lower HGH levels.

Refined carbs and sugar raise insulin levels the most, so reducing your intake may help optimize growth hormone levels.

One study found that healthy people had 3–4 times higher HGH levels than those with diabetes, as well as impaired carb tolerance and insulin function.

Along with directly affecting insulin levels, excess sugar intake is a key factor in weight gain and obesity, which also affect HGH levels.

That said, the occasional sweet treat will not impact your HGH levels in the long term.

Aim to achieve a balanced diet, as what you eat has a profound effect on your health, hormones, and body composition.

Don't eat a lot before bedtime

Your body naturally releases significant amounts of HGH, especially at night.

Given that most meals cause a rise in insulin levels, some experts suggest avoiding food before bedtime.

In particular, a high-carb or high-protein meal may spike your insulin and potentially block some of the HGH released at night.

Keep in mind that insufficient research exists on this theory.

Nevertheless, insulin levels normally decrease 2–3 hours after eating, so you may wish to avoid carb- or protein-based meals 2–3 hours before bedtime.

Take a GABA supplement

Gamma aminobutyric acid (GABA) is a non-protein amino acid that functions as a neurotransmitter, sending signals around your brain.

As a well-known calming agent for your brain and central nervous system, it's often used to aid sleep. Interestingly, it may also help increase your HGH levels.

One study found that taking a GABA supplement led to a 400% increase in HGH at rest and a 200% increase following exercise.

GABA may also increase HGH levels by improving your sleep, since your nighttime growth hormone release is linked to sleep quality and depth.

However, most of these increases were short-lived and GABA's long-term benefits for growth hormone levels remain unclear.

Exercise at a high intensity

Exercise is one of the most effective ways to significantly raise your HGH levels.

The increase depends on the type of exercise, intensity, food intake around the workout, and your body's own traits.

High-intensity exercise increases HGH the most, but all forms of exercise are beneficial.

You can perform repeated sprints, interval training, weight training, or circuit training to spike your HGH levels and maximize fat loss.

As with supplements, exercise mainly causes short-term spikes in HGH levels.

Nevertheless, over the long term, exercise may optimize your hormone function and decrease body fat, both of which will benefit your HGH levels.

Take beta-alanine and/or a sports drink around your workouts

Some sports supplements can optimize performance and temporarily boost your HGH levels.

In one study, taking 4.8 grams of beta-alanine before a workout increased the number of repetitions performed by 22%

It also doubled peak power and boosted HGH levels compared with the non-supplement group.

Another study demonstrated that a sugary sports drink increased HGH levels toward the end of a workout.

However, if you're trying to lose fat, the drink's extra calories will negate any benefit from the short-term HGH spike.

Studies have shown that protein shakes —both with and without carbs — can boost HGH levels around workouts.

However, if a casein or whey protein supplement is taken immediately before strength exercise, it may have the opposite effect.

One study found that drinking a beverage containing 25 grams (0.9 ounces) of casein or whey protein 30 minutes before strength exercise reduced levels of human growth hormone and testosterone, compared with a non-caloric placebo.

Optimize your sleep

The majority of HGH is released in pulses when you sleep. These pulses are based on your body's internal clock or circadian rhythm.

The largest pulses occur before midnight, with some smaller pulses in the early morning.

Studies have shown that poor sleep can reduce the amount of HGH your body produces.

In fact, getting an adequate amount of deep sleep is one of the best strategies to enhance your long-term HGH production.

Here are a few simple strategies to help optimize your sleep:

- Avoid blue light exposure before bedtime
- Read a book in the evening
- Make sure your bedroom is at a comfortable temperature
- Don't consume caffeine late in the day

Take a melatonin supplement

Melatonin is a hormone that plays an important role in sleep and blood pressure regulation.

Melatonin supplements have become a popular sleep aid that can increase the quality and duration of your sleep.

While good sleep alone may benefit HGH levels, further research has shown that a melatonin supplement can directly enhance HGH production.

Melatonin is also fairly safe and non-toxic. However, it may alter your brain chemistry in some ways, so you may want to check with your healthcare provider before using it.

To maximize its effects, take 1–5 mg about 30 minutes before bed. Start with a lower dose to assess your tolerance, then increase if needed.

Take other natural supplements

Several other supplements may enhance human growth hormone production, including:

- Glutamine. A 2-gram dose may temporarily increase levels up to 78%
- Creatine. A 20-gram dose of creatine significantly increased HGH levels for 2–6 hours
- Ornithine. One study gave participants ornithine 30 minutes after exercise and found a greater peak in HGH levels
- L-dopa. In patients with Parkinson's disease, 500 mg of L-dopa increased HGH levels for up to 2 hours
- Glycine. Studies have found glycine can improve gym performance and provide short-term spikes in HGH

While these supplements may increase your HGH levels, studies indicate that their effects are only temporary.

8 Testosterone-Boosting Foods

Testosterone is a male sex hormone that affects more than just sex drive. The hormone is also responsible for:

- bone and muscle health
- sperm production
- hair growth

You can lose testosterone as you age, as well as from chronic illnesses. Hypogonadism, also called low testosterone or low T, is often medically treated to prevent future health problems.

An overall balancing of hormones is important to manage testosterone levels. This means consuming a well-balanced, nutrient-dense diet.

Being mindful of the total intake of foods containing hormones or hormone-mimicking nutrients, such as phytoestrogens, is recommended to achieve improved testosterone levels.

Some studies have shown these nutrients may have an effect on overall hormone balance.

Along with your doctor's recommendations, you may consider potential testosterone-boosting foods as a natural complement to low T treatments.

Two nutrients that are especially important to your diet are vitamin D and zinc, both of which are precursors for making testosterone. This article will focus on the foods highlighting these two nutrients.

1. Tuna

Tuna is rich in vitamin D, which has been linked to a longer life and testosterone production. It's also a heart-healthy, protein-rich food that's low in calories.

Whether you choose canned or fresh, eating this fish can be a natural way of boosting testosterone. A serving of tuna fulfills your daily vitamin D needs.

If you aren't a tuna fan, you may consider other fishy sources of vitamin D, such as salmon or sardines.

Remember that moderation is key. Aim for a max of two to three servings a week to minimize your intake of mercury, which is found in seafood.

2. Low-fat milk with vitamin D

Milk is a great source of protein and calcium.

Children and women are encouraged to drink milk for better bone health, but milk can also keep men's bones strong too. The vitamin D content may also keep testosterone levels in check.

Make sure you choose milk that's fortified with vitamin D. Choose low fat or skim versions. They have the same nutrients as whole milk without all of the saturated fat.

3. Egg yolks

Egg yolks are another rich source of vitamin D.

While cholesterol has a bad reputation, egg yolk contains more nutrients than egg whites.

The cholesterol of egg yolks may even help low T. As long as you don't have any preexisting cholesterol issues, you can safely eat one egg per day.

4. Fortified cereals

Eggs aren't the only breakfast food that can help low T. If you have to watch your blood cholesterol, this is especially good news.

Certain cereal brands are fortified with vitamin D, not to mention other heart-healthy nutrients. Consider incorporating fortified cereals into your breakfast routine to jump-start your day and your testosterone levels.

5. Oysters

Zinc is an essential nutrient during puberty, and its effects can keep male hormones in check throughout adulthood.

Men who have low T benefit from increasing their zinc intake if they also have zinc deficiencies. Oysters are good sources of this mineral.

6. Shellfish

An occasional serving of crab or lobster may do your testosterone levels some good. This is thanks in part to the zinc content in these seafood favorites.

According to the National Institutes of Health, Alaskan king crab has 43 percent of your daily value of zinc in just a 3-ounce serving.

7. Beef

There are real health concerns about the overconsumption of red meat. Not only do some cuts have more fat than poultry, but eating too much is also linked to certain cancers, such as colon cancer.

Still, some cuts of beef have nutrients that can boost testosterone. Beef liver is an exceptional source of vitamin D, while ground beef and chuck roast contain zinc.

To keep animal fats in check, choose only lean cuts of beef and avoid eating it every day.

8. Beans

When it comes to male hormone health, beans may offer more benefits than you think. Many legumes, such as chickpeas, lentils, and baked beans, are all considered good sources of zinc.

As a bonus, these foods are full of fiber and plant-based proteins that can protect your heart health.

More Food for Thought

Healthy diet changes may help with low T, but they're not cures for hypogonadism. A doctor must confirm that you have low testosterone through a physical exam and blood test.

If you're diagnosed with low T, you may be prescribed testosterone hormone replacements, such as:

- tablets or pills
- skin patches
- topical gel
- injections

These medications can also come with the risk of serious side effects, so make sure you discuss all of them with your doctor beforehand.

Additionally, consider making dietary adjustments to boost your overall health, not just to treat low T.

Growth Hormone Deficiency

A growth hormone deficiency (GHD) occurs when the pituitary gland doesn't produce enough growth hormone. It more commonly affects children than adults.

The pituitary gland is a small gland about the size of a pea. It's located at the base of the skull and secretes eight hormones. Some of these hormones control thyroid activity and body temperature.

GHD occurs in roughly 1 in 7,000 births. The condition is also a symptom of several genetic diseases, including Turner syndrome and Prader-Willi syndrome.

You may grow concerned if your child is not meeting height and weight growth standards. Growth hormone deficiency is treatable. Children who are diagnosed early often recover very well. If left untreated, the condition can result in shorter-than-average height and delayed puberty.

Your body still needs growth hormones after you've finished puberty. Once you're in adulthood, the growth hormone maintains your body structure and metabolism. Adults can also develop GHD, but it isn't as common.

What Causes Growth Hormone Deficiency

Children with cleft lips or cleft palates often have poorly developed pituitary glands, so they are more likely to have GHD.

GHD that isn't present at birth may be caused by a tumor in the brain. These tumors are normally located at the site of the pituitary gland or the nearby hypothalamus region of the brain.

In children and adults, serious head injuries, infections, and radiation treatments can also cause GHD. This is called acquired growth hormone deficiency (AGHD).

Symptoms of Growth Hormone Deficiency

Children with GHD are shorter than their peers and have younger, rounder faces. They may also be chubby or have "baby fat" around the abdomen, even though their body proportions are normal.

If GHD develops later in a child's life, such as from a brain injury or tumor, its main symptom is delayed puberty. In some instances, sexual development is halted.

Many teens with GHD experience low self-esteem due to developmental delays such as short stature or a slow rate of maturing. For example, young women may not develop breasts and young men's voices may not change at the same rate as their peers.

Reduced bone strength is another symptom of AGHD. This may lead to more frequent fractures, especially in older adults. People with low growth hormone levels may feel tired and lack stamina. They may experience sensitivity to hot or cold temperatures.

A variety of psychological symptoms can occur, including:

- depression
- lack of concentration
- poor memory
- bouts of anxiety or emotional distress

Adults with AGHD typically have high levels of fat in the blood and high cholesterol. This isn't due to poor diet, but rather to changes in the body's metabolism caused by low levels of growth hormone. Adults with AGHD are at greater risk for diabetes and heart disease.

How is Growth Hormone Deficiency Diagnosed?

Your child's doctor will look for signs of GHD if your child is not meeting their height and weight milestones. They'll ask you about your growth rate as you approached puberty, as well as your other children's growth rates. If they suspect GHD, a number of tests can confirm the diagnosis.

A blood test can measure growth hormone in the body. However, your levels of growth hormone fluctuate widely throughout the day and night (called "diurnal variation"). A blood test with a lower-than-normal result is not enough evidence to make a diagnosis.

Growth plates are the developing tissue at each end of your arm and leg bones. Growth plates fuse together when you've finished developing. X-rays of your child's hand can indicate their level of bone growth.

Kidney and thyroid function tests can determine how the body is producing and using hormones.

If your doctor suspects a tumor or other damage to the pituitary gland, an MRI imaging scan can provide a detailed look inside the brain. Growth hormone levels will often be screened in adults who have a history of pituitary disorders, have a brain injury, or need brain surgery.

Testing can determine if the pituitary condition was present at birth or brought on by an injury or tumor.

How is Growth Hormone Deficiency Treated?

Since the mid-1980s, synthetic growth hormones have been used with great success to treat children and adults. Before synthetic growth hormones, natural growth hormones from cadavers were used for treatment.

Growth hormone is given by injection, typically into the body's fatty tissues, such as the back of the arms, thighs, or buttocks. It's most effective as a daily treatment.

Side effects are generally minor, but may include:

- redness at the injection site
- headaches

- hip pain
- curving of the spine (scoliosis)

In rare cases, long-term growth hormone injections may contribute to the development of diabetes, especially in people with a family history of that disease.

Long-Term Treatment

Children with congenital GHD are often treated with growth hormones until they reach puberty. Often, children who have too little growth hormone in their youth will naturally begin to produce enough as they enter adulthood.

However, some remain in treatment for their entire lives. Your doctor can determine if you need ongoing injections by monitoring hormone levels in your blood.

How to Stimulate Hormones for Bodybuilding

Several hormones play a critical role in bodybuilding and strength training. Testosterone, growth hormone (GH), and insulin-like growth factor (IGF-1) increase strength and stimulate muscle growth.

Other hormones such as cortisol, epinephrine, norepinephrine, and glucagon increase the availability of glucose, your body's primary source of fuel. Finally, insulin facilitates the storage of glucose in muscles for future use.

All of these hormones are part of the body's natural endocrine response. If your goal is to gain muscle mass, there are ways to stimulate hormone production without the need of illegal supplements.

Key Hormones in Bodybuilding

Muscle growth and strength are influenced by hormones in different ways. When it comes to bodybuilding, some specifically promote muscle growth, while others influence the way we use and store glucose for training and competition.

Testosterone

Testosterone is a male hormone produced mainly by the testicles but also by the adrenal glands situated on top of the kidneys.

Testosterone is responsible for the development of male physical characteristics, muscle mass, strength, fat distribution, and sex drive. In women, testosterone is produced by the ovaries and adrenal glands, albeit in lower quantities.

Testosterone is classified as both an androgenic and anabolic steroid hormone. Androgenic refers to male characteristics, while the term anabolic refers to the growth of body tissue. Testosterone is arguably the most important hormone for bodybuilding, although the amount the body produces will gradually wane as we get older.

The use of supplementary anabolic steroids to build muscle has been popular for decades. They work spectacularly but are also known to carry potentially serious health risks. It is for this reason that any form of testosterone supplementation is banned in sports.

Growth Hormone and IGF-1

Growth hormone is produced by the pituitary gland and stimulates the liver to produce IGF-1, the hormone ultimately responsible for anabolic muscle growth. As with testosterone, the production of GH declines as we age. Both hormones have an inverse relationship to body fat, meaning that the less GH and IGF-1 you produce, the more body fat you will accumulate.

Insulin

Insulin is the storage hormone produced by the pancreas in response to food. When food is eaten, it is broken down into glucose, fatty acids, amino acids, vitamins, and minerals.

Insulin responds by warehousing the stored form of glucose, known as glycogen, in muscles and the liver. It also enables amino acids to repair damaged tissues and build muscle mass.

These effects are considered anabolic. Insulin production is largely influenced by exercise and diet, especially the consumption of carbohydrates and protein.

Cortisol

Cortisol is produced by the adrenal glands and is often called the "stress hormone" because its release is triggered by physical and/or emotional stress.

Cortisol is a catabolic hormone, meaning that it breaks down tissue. In addition to controlling inflammation, cortisol makes glucose available by breaking down muscle whenever the blood sugar is low.

This commonly occurs during endurance sports when the circulating glucose supply has been used up.

Hydrocortisone and cortisone are the manufactured forms of cortisol.

Epinephrine

Epinephrine (adrenaline) is called the "fight or flight" hormone because it acts quickly at times of stress to constrict arteries and raise blood pressure. This increases your heart rate to deliver oxygen more effectively. Epinephrine also constricts airways so that respiration is more efficient.

On top of this, epinephrine directs the muscles and liver to surrender their glucose stores during strenuous activity. In this sense, epinephrine is a catabolic hormone like cortisol.

Glucagon

Glucagon acts like a mirror hormone of insulin. When you fast or eat a low-carb diet, glucagon responds more efficiently than insulin to replenish low glucose supplies.

Glucagon works by instructing the liver to give up its glucose stores. It also breaks down muscles to increase cortisol, which stimulates the production of glucose. If insulin is considered anabolic, then glucagon is catabolic.

How to Enhance Hormones Naturally

There are several approaches to diet and training that can enhance the anabolic response while mitigating the catabolic response.

Pre- and Post-Exercise Nutrition

The foods you eat before, during, and after exercise can make a big difference in your training.

For example, eating carbohydrates before and during exercise can help minimize increases in cortisol. The reason is simple: when your blood glucose supplies are maintained, cortisol does not need to be released and your muscle tissues won't get burned up.

It is important to note that exercise also increases testosterone levels. Once exercise stops, testosterone will invariably drop as cortisone levels rise. To mitigate this effect, you need to eat protein after a workout to balance the testosterone-to-cortisone ratio in your bloodstream.

Here are some tips that can help:

Consume 20 grams of easily digested protein up to 45 minutes before a workout. Around 20 fluid ounces (600 milliliters) of skim milk with a little sugar will do.

Sip a sports drink during workouts at regular intervals, especially if you go beyond 60 minutes.

Within 30 minutes of completing your workout, consume another 20 grams of protein with around 40 grams of carbohydrate. Again, skim milk with sugar works just fine. Choose your favorite protein-carb powder or protein-fortified milk drink.

Your carb-to-protein ratio should be between 3:1 and 4:1 if you have had a heavy workout.

Macronutrient Composition

Eating a diet that's neither too low in fat nor too high in protein can help enhance your testosterone output.

contrast, ultra low-fat diets (like the Pritikin or Ornish diet) or high-protein/low-carb diets are not advised when bodybuilding.

Protein Intake

Some bodybuilders endorse diets comprised of 40 percent protein. Not only is there little evidence to support this strategy, but it may also cause harm over the long term, increasing the risk of kidney damage and proteinuria.

Workout Strategies

High-intensity training raises testosterone, GH, and IGF-1 levels but also promotes spikes in cortisol. While diet can temper cortisol production to a certain extent, how you exercise may also help.

High-volume, high-intensity workouts with short rest intervals tend to produce the greatest increases in testosterone, GH, and cortisol, while low-volume, high-intensity workouts with long rest intervals tend to produce the least.

Doing so appears to restore a high-energy compound known as phosphagen that is stored in muscles and excreted during strenuous activity. It also promotes the production of testosterone with less of the mitigating effects of cortisone. So, in a way, you can get more out of your training by pushing less strenuously.

Other Tips

Aerobic training, like running or anaerobic interval training, should be done on separate days from your bodybuilding training. Doing both on the same day promotes inflammation and the adverse effects of cortisol.

Evening workouts are preferable to early-morning workouts since cortisol levels tend to peak in the early hours of the day.

Alcohol consumption increases cortisol production and should be avoided during heavy training and competition.

Improved sleep hygiene, including maintaining a regular sleep schedule, enhances the production of GH, which peaks during deep sleep and can persist well after waking. By contrast, irregular sleep contributes to drops in GH levels.

Foods that Lower Testosterone Levels

Here are 8 foods that lower testosterone levels you may want to watch out for.

1. Soy and Soy-Based Products

Some research shows that regularly eating soy products like edamame, tofu, soy milk and miso may cause a drop in testosterone levels.

For example, one study in 35 men found that drinking soy protein isolate for 54 days resulted in decreased testosterone levels.

Soy foods are also high in phytoestrogens, which are plant-based substances that mimic the effects of estrogen in your body by altering hormone levels and potentially reducing testosterone.

Though human-based research is limited, one rat study showed that consuming phytoestrogens significantly decreased testosterone levels and prostate weight.

However, other research found conflicting results, suggesting that soy-based foods may not have as much of an impact as these isolated soy components.

In fact, one large review of 15 studies found that soy foods had no effect on testosterone levels in men.

Further research is needed to understand how soy products as a whole may influence testosterone levels in humans.

2. Mint

Perhaps most well-known for its powerful stomach-soothing properties, some research suggests that mint could cause a dip in testosterone levels.

In particular, spearmint and peppermint — two herbs that hail from the mint family of plants — have been shown to have a direct impact on testosterone.

One 30-day study in 42 women showed that drinking spearmint herbal tea daily caused a significant decline in testosterone levels.

Similarly, an animal study found that administering spearmint essential oil to rats for 20 days resulted in reduced testosterone levels.

Meanwhile, another animal study noted that drinking peppermint tea altered hormone levels in rats, leading to a decrease in testosterone, compared to a control group.

However, most research on mint and testosterone focuses on women or animals.

High-quality human studies focusing on both genders are needed to assess how mint affects testosterone levels in both men and women.

3. Licorice Root

Licorice root is an ingredient commonly used to sweeten candies and beverages.

It's also a popular natural remedy in holistic medicine and often used to treat everything from chronic pain to persistent coughing.

In recent years, several studies have found that licorice may also influence hormone levels, potentially leading to a decline in testosterone over time.

In one study, 25 men consumed 7 grams of licorice root daily, which caused a 26% drop in testosterone levels after just one week.

Another small study showed that licorice may reduce testosterone levels in women as well, reporting that 3.5 grams of licorice daily decreased testosterone levels by 32% after just one menstrual cycle.

Keep in mind that this applies to licorice root rather than licorice candy, which often doesn't contain any licorice root.

4. Vegetable Oil

Many of the most common vegetable oils, including canola, soybean, corn and cottonseed oil, are loaded with polyunsaturated fatty acids.

These fatty acids are usually classified as a healthy source of dietary fat, but they may also decrease testosterone levels, as several studies have suggested.

One study in 69 men showed that frequently consuming polyunsaturated fats was associated with significantly lower testosterone levels.

Another study in 12 men looked at the effects of diet on testosterone levels after exercise and reported that polyunsaturated fat intake was linked to lower levels of testosterone.

However, recent research is limited, and most studies are observational with a small sample size.

More high-quality studies are needed to examine the effects of vegetable oils on testosterone levels in the general population.

5. Flaxseed

Flaxseed is packed with heart-healthy fats, fiber and various important vitamins and minerals.

In addition, some research shows that it may cause a decrease in testosterone levels.

This is because flaxseed is high in lignans, which are plant compounds that bind to testosterone and force it to be excreted from your body.

What's more, flaxseed is rich in omega-3 fatty acids, which may be linked to a decrease in testosterone as well.

In one small study in 25 men with prostate cancer, supplementing with flaxseed and decreasing overall fat intake was shown to significantly reduce testosterone levels.

Similarly, a case study reported daily flaxseed supplements decreased testosterone levels in a 31-year-old woman with polycystic ovary syndrome, a condition characterized by increased male hormones in women.

However, more large-scale studies are needed to further evaluate the effects of flaxseed on testosterone levels.

6. Processed Foods

Besides often being high in sodium, calories, and added sugar, processed foods like convenience meals, frozen foods, and pre-packaged snacks are also a common source of trans fats.

Trans fats, an unhealthy type of fat have been linked to an increased risk of heart disease, type 2 diabetes and inflammation.

Plus, some studies have found that regularly consuming trans fats from sources like processed foods could decrease testosterone levels.

For example, one study in 209 men showed that those who consumed the highest amounts of trans fats had 15% lower levels of testosterone than those with the lowest intake.

Additionally, they also had a 37% lower sperm count and a decrease in testicular volume, which may be linked to reduced testicular function.

Animal studies have also found that a high intake of trans fats could lower testosterone levels and even impair reproductive performance.

7. Alcohol

While enjoying the occasional glass of wine with dinner has been linked to health benefits, studies show that excessive alcohol intake could cause testosterone levels to plummet especially in men.

A study in 19 healthy adults showed that consuming 30–40 grams of alcohol per day, which equates to about 2–3 standard drinks, decreased testosterone levels in men by 6.8% over three weeks.

Another study reported that acute alcohol intoxication was associated with increased testosterone in women but decreased levels in men.

However, the evidence isn't completely clear-cut when it comes to the effects of alcohol on testosterone.

In fact, both human and animal studies have had mixed results, with some research indicating that alcohol could actually increase testosterone levels in certain cases.

Further research is still needed to understand how different doses of alcohol affect testosterone levels in the general population.

8. Nuts

Nuts are a great source of many important nutrients, including fiber, heart-healthy fats, and minerals like folic acid, selenium, and magnesium.

Additionally, some studies suggest that certain types of nuts may decrease testosterone levels.

One small study in 31 women with polycystic ovary syndrome showed that walnuts and almonds increased levels of sex hormone-binding globulin (SHBG) by 12.5% and 16%, respectively.

SHBG is a type of protein that binds to testosterone, which can lead to a decrease in the levels of free testosterone in your body.

Nuts are also generally high in polyunsaturated fatty acids, which have been associated with decreased testosterone levels in some studies.

Despite these findings, more research is needed to determine how certain types of nuts may impact testosterone levels.

The Bottom Line

Changing up your diet is one of the most effective ways to maintaining healthy testosterone levels.

If you're concerned about low testosterone levels, swapping out these testosterone-lowering foods and replacing them with healthy, whole food alternatives can keep levels in check and enhance your overall health.

Additionally, maintaining a healthy lifestyle, getting plenty of sleep and fitting exercise into your routine are some other significant steps you can take to naturally boost testosterone.

Chapter 7 Summary

Your hormones are just as important to building muscle mass as the training itself.

Stick to the recommended diet and supplements to get the best results!

Chapter 8: How to Dress to Match Your New Body

So, you're all carved up and your body looks great. This means you don't need your old clothes anymore. You should wear clothes that'll do justice to that broad chest, well-built biceps, and super-sexy abs.

Fitted outfits are best for revealing your new-found physique to the world. The ladies will love it, and so would you whenever you look in the mirror or receive those heartwarming compliments.

You may not be a fashion-minded person, so you may be confused as to which types of clothes you should wear. Not to worry, I'll be recommending just what you need!

Suit Buying Tips for Muscular Men

Suits are great, they bring out the executive side of you. They also make you look a lot more serious and sharp.

For bodybuilders who are in the corporate world, finding the right suit may be a challenge, since their bodies are unlike those of the general male population.

Bodybuilders have chests, shoulders and arms that are much broader. They also have slimmer waists, as well as thicker legs. So you see, you can't just buy any suit off the rack, you have to pick the right ones that'll match your physique!

Let me share with you some tips on how to get the best suit for your muscular physique.

Off The Rack (OTR) vs. Made to Measure (MTM)

For best results, I strongly recommend that muscular men go for Made-To-Measure suits, as opposed to buying Off-The-Rack.

Remember, I pointed out that a muscular man's body doesn't measure up the same with that of the average man, all thanks to better built physical features. Most suits you will find in shops are made for out of shape or overweight men, and not for you.

So, you most likely will not find the right fitting when you go to a store to shop for a suit.

Made-To-Measure suits will fit you better since they are made specifically with your dimensions in mind. Your tailor will take all specific measurements and make your suit accordingly, giving you the perfect fit that your new body deserves.

Another advantage of MTM suits is that you can determine the quality of the materials you want for your suit. This is unlike buying off-the-rack, where you will have to settle for the materials you find.

MTM suits may cost you more, or less, depending on the materials you select. I expect that you go for top quality fabrics, as you would want your suit to last as long as it can.

If you must buy a suit from a store, then you should buy a suit separately. That is, suits where the jackets and trousers are sold separately. This will make your job a lot easier.

For the jacket, look for one that fits your chest and shoulder dimensions. As for the trousers, scout for one that fits you all through your seat and thighs. Then, find a good tailor to handle the rest.

Soft or Natural Shoulders vs. Padded Shoulders

Muscular guys are usually blessed with larger shoulders, so it would be wise to pay attention to how your jacket fits those areas. Since your shoulders are large, you wouldn't be needing your jacket to have excessive padding, as that would only make you look like an outrageously built superhero from a comic book.

Your muscle mass is enough, so the extra padding is a bad idea!

Go for what is commonly called "soft shoulder" or "natural shoulder" jackets.

Remember you are already in great shape, so your clothes don't need to do the lifting for you, your well-built body can take care of that all by itself!

The less padding, the better the fit for your shoulders.

Waist Suppression

This is another area where muscular men may find challenging – The waist of the jacket!

The reason why this area is so problematic is that there is a large difference between the chest and waist measurements.

It is rather common to find bodybuilders having as high as a 10-inch drop between their chest and waist measurements. If you belong to this group of men, you need to be careful when your tailor factors in the waist of your jacket.

You would want to make sure your jacket's waist isn't too boxy, you would also want to avoid having too much waist suppression. Once again, a good and trusted tailor who knows his onions is the person to call on.

Finding Trousers for Muscular Thighs

All the work you put in at the gym didn't just build your arms, back, and chest, it built your thighs too, and larger sized thighs can be an issue when picking out trousers.

I have mentioned before that buying suit separates is your best bet. This would mean sizing up in the trouser so you can create more space in the thigh. Then, you can have your tailor take in the waist.

For those with really large thighs, sizing up may not solve the problem. You can have your tailor let the thighs out on your trousers in order to give your hamstrings and quads some extra room.

This may not work for all trousers, so make sure there is some extra material in the thigh that you can have let out before making your purchase.

Follow these tips and you will get the right suit fitting for your unique, muscular physique!

Jeans Buying Tips for Men with Muscular Thighs

All the squats you threw in at the gym has changed the anatomy of your thighs, as you'd expect. Muscle mass has been built-up and your old pairs of jeans just can't fit anymore.

So, for the lovers of jeans out there, I'll be giving you some tips which would be helpful in getting the right jeans for your muscular thighs.

The Problem

When you're on the lookout for jeans, you'll notice that if the hips and thighs are a perfect fit, the leg openings and the waist will be too large.

This is because most jeans are made for regular-looking men, and not for you. The designers usually make the hip, waist, and leg opening size proportionate to a general size, and not for men with thick hips.

On the other hand, of the leg has the kind of taper you are looking for, you will find that you wouldn't be able to get the jeans beyond your knees.

Also, if you manage to squeeze yourself into a pair, they would be pretty tight and would cause you a great deal of discomfort when you put them on. This discomfort is more pronounced when you sit, all thanks to a limited range of motion, which requires you to naturally round your back.

Don't be mad at the manufacturers, it really isn't their fault. After all, lean muscular guys such as yourself are a minority, so it is expected that they cater to the larger population who have a fit.

If it makes you feel any better, consider yourself as a special breed, one that is unique, and who stands out from the crowd. Because really, that's what you are!

Now that you understand the challenges involved, permit me to give you some tips on how a muscular man like you can get the perfect fit for jeans.

Getting the Right Fit for Jeans

Similar to the dilemma you would face when buying suits, buying the right pair of jeans off the rack would be challenging.

Here's what you can do.

Tailoring

Custom tailoring isn't limited to suits alone, why should they?

You can hire the services of a top-draw tailor to give you the perfect fitting for jeans. This may cost you more, but consider this – Don't you think having 3 to 4 pairs of jeans that fit is a much better deal than having 10 pairs that don't?

Your answer is as good as mine!

However, before you have your jeans tailored, consider these first.

Find the right tailor: Do not make the mistake of handing your denim to just any tailor. First, find a tailor who would listen to your complaints and help you find solutions that are unique to your thighs.

A lot of tailors out there don't pay special attention to your needs and will proceed to make alterations as they normally do.

Be sure to tell your tailor exactly what you want, and make sure he understands the problem if not, you will not get what you are looking for.

Wash or soak before alterations: I can only imagine how sad you would be if you have your denim tailored to fit, only for them to shrink to an unfitting size after the first wash!

Washing or soaking them before you have them tailored is your best bet. If they shrink, then your tailor will make alterations accordingly.

Don't forget to do this, as it is vital to your fitting. It will also save you the heartache of wasting money.

Tailoring Option A

Be sure to buy one or two sizes up, then have the waist taken in. Buying a straight type of jean a few sizes up will give you a good fit in the hips, thighs, and ankles.

This however will leave you with a massive waistband, and you may be tempted to cinch it up with your belt.

But there is a better option. Take them to a trusted tailor and have the waist taken in.

This alteration is pretty simple and straightforward, so you're tailor shouldn't have any problems here.

Keep in mind however, that alterations can cause a few proportions such as the spacing between the back pockets to become wonky if you remove more than 2 inches from the waist.

Tailoring Option B

Buy relaxed fit and then have the legs tapered.

For a muscular guy, you should consider yourself lucky if you can find a pair of jeans that fit your thighs, waist, and hips, as these are all too rare to come about. Being baggy from the knee down shouldn't be much of a problem, as your tailor can easily alter the legs.

Be certain of the fitting you want before you buy your jeans. An extra tip is to buy a pair that fits you well enough at the ankle area, then lie flat and measure the hem.

Keep in mind that most tailors don't have vast experience working with muscular men, some have never even worked with muscular men at all, so you need to be very certain of what you want, and make it clear to your tailor.

One more thing, if you bought selvage denims and you'd like to preserve the original outseam, make your request clear to your tailor that the alterations should be made to the inseam.

Consider Stretchy Denims

Have you considered buying denim with a built-in stretch? Yeah I know, most denim lovers don't even want to consider the option of wearing stretchy denims. After all, jeans are meant to be tough, rugged, and should display masculinity. Stretchy denims defeats this purpose, so I totally understand how you feel.

Not to worry, your take on stretches may change, sooner than later.

Being a guy with an athletic physique, you can find a pair of jeans at a store that has one to two percent elastic, and they would fit just right.

Pairs like these won't give you the same feeling as the traditional rugged denims, but hey, you'd be free to move and squat just as you please without any discomfort.

Give Your Denims Time

The general idea when shopping for denims is to get unique creases and fades that fit to your body. Infrequent washing is what you should consider.

When your raw denim is washed and dried less regularly than normal, they will have the chance to stretch a little bit.

Keep in mind that all denims are not the same, but if you manage to fit into a pair, then they are big enough, as they would stretch to a fit that suits you after you've worn them a few times.

Soak the Trouble Areas

You must have come across suggestions that advise you wear your jeans while they are wet, then do some squats in a bid to achieve the perfect fit. Sounds like a plan, but you may be less than impressed with the results.

My first attempt at wearing raw denim was when I bought a pair of Levi's Shrink to Fits. After I soaked it the first time, I stuck with the popular advice of squatting in them while they were still wet.

I put in the work, and I expected the thigh area would be stretched out just right.

Wrong! The results I got from squatting in soaked jeans were just terrible!

I found that the knees were dried and they took a ridiculous bulbous shape. Also, the seat was stretched out like a bloated, saggy diaper!

Yeah, the thighs were stretched, but not in the fashion I was hoping for. This prompted me to soak them again, hoping that the overstretched parts would shrink down.

I made a second attempt, and I decided I should let the jeans shrink completely, wear them when they were dried, then soak just the problematic areas. I used a spray bottle for this, as it made it easy to exclusively target the outstretched areas.

Guess what? It worked like magic!

I succeeded in stretching the hips and thighs and kept the knees, waist, and seat as they were originally.

The good news is, you can perform this procedure on any denim, not just the raw types.

All you are required to do is to soak the areas that are tight, then throw in some physical activity to trigger your desired fitting. These include squatting, sitting, and walking around for a while.

After you've done as many movements as required, proceed to hang them to dry.

This technique works perfectly well if you don't wash frequently. Unless of course, you have the time to turn it to a weekly routine.

Best Jeans for Muscular Legs

So, you'd like to kick off with a pair that is close to perfect as possible. Below are a few recommendations.

GAP 1969 Japanese Selvedge in straight fit: These jeans are perfect for men with athletic, but not necessarily large thighs. At first, you may find them to be tight around the hips and thighs, but after wearing them a couple of times, they would stretch out to a comfortable fit.

What I love most about these jeans is that the ankles aren't as bogus as other straight-legged jeans.

You can wear this pair without the need for alteration, as long as you let the hips and thighs stretch out. Also, minimize washing for best results.

Levi's 550 relaxed fit jeans: If you're looking for room in the seat and thigh, then these jeans may be just what you need. One minor issue though, you may find some bagginess just below the knees.

If you need a taper, then just follow the tips I've dropped above and hire a tailor that has some experience at altering denim.

Levi's 541 athletic fit: These jeans are made from 99% cotton and 1% elastane.

You may wonder what much difference 1% elastane would make. Well, a lot!

When I first put on my true-waist size, they hugged my hips and thighs more than I would like. At first, I thought it would be impossible to move freely in a pair like this, but it wasn't, not by any means!

I took a few slight bends, and to my greatest surprise, there was little to no resistance. I did a few parallel squats, and voila! I could still move freely!

Keep in mind, I am talking about skin-tight jeans here!

If you're a large muscular guy, then find the size that best suits your extra body mass.

Barbell Apparel Straight Athletic Fit: If you're a denim purist who doesn't have the time or willingness to go for alterations or stretching, then this pair is just right for you!

Until the Barbell Apparel, you couldn't find a pair of denims made specifically for bodybuilders. If you did, then they would have been well below par, as this pair redefined denims for muscular men.

The only denim that catered to bodybuilders back then was the JNCO jeans, and trust me, I never considered them good enough.

All that has changed with the Advent of the Barbell Apparel. It doesn't matter how muscular you are, you could walk into a store and buy a pair straight off the rack and look good in them.

I have to mention though, you'll have to do without the patches, rhinestones, and of course the embroidery.

It's true they aren't the raw selvage you prefer, but you have to make do with this. Unless you no longer want those huge, bulky legs anymore.

A little compromise won't hurt!

Food for Thought

Think of it like this, all the hard work has been done in the gym to get your legs to the physique they are in, and that's not a piece of cake. So, finding a pair of jeans that fit should be a laughable task, as it is a gazillion times easier to do.

Going by all the tips, stretching techniques, and the brands I've suggested above, even men with the most hulk-like thighs would be able to find or create a pair of denims that fit. It only takes 3 things.

- Knowing what you want
- A little effort
- Patience

It doesn't matter if you want to stretch out your pair, have them tailored, or just buy a pair of Barbells, there's a solution to every type, and size of muscular hips!

T-shirts for Bodybuilders

Nothing pops out the outline of your chest and biceps better than a fitted t-shirt. Trust me, the ladies would love your looks when you step out in a clean, well-textured, fitted tee!

Tees aren't just great for showing off all the hard work you've been putting in, they are also among the most comfortable pieces of casual clothing you can ever put on.

Below, I'll be recommending some really nice t-shirts which you can wear to the beach, the gym, or for a casual outing.

Gildan Crew T-Shirts

These tees are super comfy and they will rest well on your chest and biceps. They absorb moisture in will keep you cool all through your workout.

They are also great for the summer, as it absorbs heat for as long as you have it on. They are also built to last and can be machine-washed. What's more, they are designed with a durable tubular collar, so there's no chance of it slacking, unless you yank them hard with those strong arms of yours. Lol.

They are a bodybuilder's favorite, you'll love it!

Muscle Alive Men's Button T-Shirt

This is another tee you would absolutely adore. Unlike the regular round-neck or V-neck tee, this one is designed with a single button closure right in the center of the front part of the collar. This makes it stylish and ideal for casual outings.

It is really soft, stretchy, and comfortable, thanks to its 95% cotton and 5% spandex build.

This fitted tee was made for muscular men, however, it comes one smaller than the regular U.S size, so be sure to buy at least one size up, as it shrinks after the first wash.

Rothco Distressed US Flag Athletic Fit T-Shirt

For those who want an athletic fitting, then I recommend this tee right here.

It is as soft as you would want a t-shirt to be, it is equally durable. All thanks to it's 60% cotton and 40% Polyester material combination.

As for stylishness, you can find a distressed US flag design right across the chest, and a reversed flag graphic across the right sleeve.

For extra comfort, this tee was made tagless, good news if you ask me.

With an athletic fit, an insert collar, a wider chest area, and smaller sleeves, this tee will bring out the beastly nature of your well-carved physique!

It may interest you to know that Rothco is the foremost supplier of military, tactical, outdoor, and surviving apparel in America. Knowing this alone will make you feel as athletic and as masculine as ever!

Neleus Men's Dry Fit Athletic Performance T-Shirt

This tee is machine washable, as it is made from 100% Polyester material.

Thanks to its fabric, you wouldn't have to worry about moisture, as it is wicked away from your skin. This means you can wear it as an under-shirt. It is also pretty soft, so you won't miss the touch of cotton.

As for breathability and ventilation, you have nothing to worry about, as this tee does well in both areas. This means you will remain cool all through your workouts or any other athletic activity. These include running and walking.

If you're the type that loves taking walk at night, then you would love its reflective logo, which makes you stand out in environments with poor lighting.

Lastly, this tee is designed to protect your skin from harmful UV rays. So don't fret if you are ever exposed to them.

C9 Champion's Men's Sleeveless Tech Tee

Made with 94% Polyester & 6% Spandex, this is one of the most comfortable tees a bodybuilder can put on.

Having a body-skimming fit, this tee will sit nicely on your masculine body.

This sleeveless moisture-wicking tee can be machine-washed, and it dries just as fast. Thanks to its breathable fabric, you will be kept cool for as long as it remains on your skin.

This makes it great for several athletic activities and training sessions. It also has a 50+ UV protection feature to spare you from the effects of harmful rays.

Russell Athletic Men's Dry Power Sleeveless Muscle Tee

This is the second sleeveless tee on my list.

It has basically the same features as the previously mentioned tee, so I guess you'd love it the same.

It offers great breathability, and it has special moisture absorbing abilities. This makes it the right piece for all your workout programs, as well as several other athletic activities such as jogging, running, walking, boxing, and weightlifting.

But that's not all, you could also match this with a pair of shorts and hit the beach!

You can surf all you want with this armless tee, and feel as comfortable and free as the wind itself. You could also put it on when you go water skiing, or participate in other beach sports.

Its quality is top-tier and you can hardly find an athletic tee better than this!

Chapter 8 Summary

You've put in months and years into training and building up your body to the enviable physique you have today. For that reason alone, you should wear clothes that fit your new body.

Your bodybuilder physique would make it tough to find the right fitting since most apparel manufacturers don't make clothes with bodybuilders in mind. However, you can still find, alter, and reshape your clothes to a perfect fit.

I trust the tips and clothing recommendations I have given you above will be of great help in finding the right clothes that will bring out the beauty of your true physique, and leave the ladies gawking!

Conclusion

There you have it! All the tips, tricks, programs, diet recommendations, and clothing advice you will need throughout the course of your bodybuilding journey.

Train right, eat right, and dress to impress!

You're most welcome!

****

If you have enjoyed reading this book, I would be very grateful if you could post an honest review. All that you need to do is to [click here](#) Then click the blue link next to the yellow stars. On the left, You'll then see a gray button that says "Write a customer review"—click that and you're good to go, thank you.

Henrik

© Copyright 2020

All Rights Reserved. No part of this book may be reproduced in any form without permission in writing from the author. Reviewers may quote brief passages in reviews.

Disclaimer: No part of this publication may be reproduced or transmitted in any form or by any means, mechanical or electronic, including photocopying or recording, or by any information storage and retrieval system, or transmitted by email without permission in writing from the publisher.

While all attempts have been made to verify the information provided in this publication, neither the author nor the publisher assumes any responsibility for errors, omissions, contrary interpretations of the subject matter herein, or liability whatsoever on behalf of the purchaser or reader of these materials.